CRIME

VICTIM

DAN BROWN

TABLE OF CONTENTS

INTRODUCTION

CRIME IN AMERICA, ACCORDING TO MEDIA SOURCES, IS ON THE RISE EVERY YEAR. EVERY AMERICAN CITIZEN EXPECTS A SAFE PLACE TO WORK AND LIVE WITHOUT THE FEAR OF BEING THE VICTIM OF A VIOLENT CRIME. THE LATEST CRIME STATISTICS, FROM THE FEDERAL GOVERNMENT, INDICATE THAT CRIME IS INCREASING EVERY YEAR. THE MURDER STATISTICS, IN THE UNITED STATES, ARE APPROACHING 20,000 VICTIMS. SEXUAL ASSAULTS EXCEED 100,000 PER YEAR. PROPERTY CRIMES (BURGLARY AND VANDALISM) ARE OVER 1,500,000 PER YEAR. LARCENCY CRIMES (PROPERTY THEFTS FROM BUSINESS AND HOME OWNERS) ARE MORE THAN 5,000,000 PER YEAR. MAJOR FELONY CRIMES ARE CONTINUING TO RISE IN EVERY STATE IN THE UNITED STATES. THE FOCUS OF THE COURTS IN THE LAST SEVERAL DECADES HAS BEEN BASED ON PROTECTING THE RIGHTS OF A CRIMINAL DEFENDANT ACCUSED OF COMMITTING THESE TYPES OF CRIMES. WHAT RIGHTS DOES THE VICTIM OF A CRIME HAVE IN AMERICAN SOCIETY? THIS PURPOSE OF THIS BOOK IS TO PROVIDE AN INSIGHT INTO THE RIGHTS OF VICTIMS OF CRIME IN OUR AMERICAN SOCIETY.

THE CRIMINAL TRIAL PROCESS

FILING OF CHARGES

ONCE THE INVESTIGATION BY LAW ENFORCEMENT AUTHORITIES IS COMPLETE, THE NEXT STEP IN THE CRIMINAL JUSTICE PROCESS IS THE FILING OF THE ACTUAL CRIMINAL CHARGES AGAINST THE PERSON OR PERSONS RESPONSIBLE FOR COMMITTING THE CRIME. THE DUTY OF FILING CRIMINAL CHARGES RESTS WITH THE UNITED STATES ATTORNEY'S OFFICE IF THE CRIME IS A FEDERAL CRIME. A CRIMINAL ACT AGAINST STATE LAW IS HANDLED BY THE ATTORNEY GENERAL OF THE STATE. ON THE LOCAL LEVEL, STATE CRIMINAL CHARGES ARE HANDLED BY THE DULY ELECTED DISTRICT ATTORNEY.

FEDERAL CRIMES

CRIMES THAT ARE A VIOLATION OF FEDERAL LAW ARE FILED IN THE UNITED STATES DISTRICT COURT WHERE THE CRIME OCCURRED. THESE CRIMES INCLUDE:

1. CRIMES ON FEDERAL PROPERTY
2. CRIMES ON TRIBAL LANDS
3. BANK ROBBERY
4. COUNTERFEITING
5. CRIMES AGAINST FEDERAL EMPLOYEES
6. ACTS OF TERRORISM
7. RACKETTEERING
8. SABOTAGE
9. TREASON

STATE CRIMES

CRIMES THAT ARE A VIOLATION OF STATE LAW ARE FILED IN THE CIRCUIT OR DISTRICT COURT WHERE THE CRIME OCCURRED. THESE CRIMES INCLUDE:

1. GRAND LARCENY
2. PETTY LARCENY
3. BURGLARY
4. ASSAULT & BATTERY
5. ARSON
6. SEX CRIMES
7. STALKING
8. DOMESTIC ABUSE
9. CHILD ABUSE
10. FRAUD (FALSE PRETENSES)
11. POSSESSION OF STOLEN PROPERTY
12. DRUNK DRIVING
13. DRUG CHARGES
14. MANSLAUGHTER
15. MURDER

PROSECUTOR DISCRETION

THE DECISION ON THE FILING OF CHARGES RESTS WITH THE PROSECUTING AUTHORITES. THE U.S. ATTORNEY MAKES THE DECISION ON FEDERAL CRIMES. THE DISTRICT ATTORNEY MAKES THE DECISION ON STATE CRIMES. BOTH FEDERAL AND STATE PROSECUTOR HAVE DISCRETION ON WHETHER TO FILE CHARGES AND THE TYPE AND NUMBER OF CHARGES TO FILE AGAINST THE DEFENDANT OR DEFENDANTS WHO COMMITTED THE CRIME.

THE FIRST HEARING

ONCE THE CHARGE(S) HAS BEEN FILED (EITHER BY AN INDICTMENT ISSUED BY A GRAND JURY IN FEDERAL COURT) OR THROUGH A COMPLAINT AND INFORMATION (FILED BY THE DISTRICT ATTORNEY IN STATE COURT), THE CHARGED DEFENDANT MUST BE BROUGHT BEFORE THE COURT FOR HIS INITIAL APPEARANCE, USUALLY CALLED THE "ARRAIGNMENT", THE FOLLOWING ITEMS ARE COVERED:

1. THE CHARGES ARE READ BY THE JUDGE;
2. THE DEFENDANT IS QUESTIONED ABOUT DOES HE OR SHE UNDERSTAND THE CHARGES;
3. THE DEFENDANT ENTER A PLEA (EITHER GUILTY OR NOT GUILTY);
4. BOND IS SET BY THE JUDGE TO ALLOW THE DEFENDANT TO BE RELEASED FROM CUSTODY UNTIL THE NEXT COURT HEARING. THE AMOUNT OF THE BOND IS DETERMINED BY THE JUDGE BASED ON THE FACTS OF THE CASE;
5. THE JUDGE DETERMINES WHETHER THE DEFENDANT HAS AN ATTORNEY. IF THE DEFENDANT CAN NOT AFFORD TO HIRE COUNSEL, THE COURT HAS TO APPOINT COUNSEL TO REPRESENT HIM IN ALL FELONY CASES;
6. THE COURT THEN SETS THE NEXT COURT HEARING, EITHER A TRIAL (MISDEMEANOR CASES) OR A PRELIMINARY HEARING IF THE CASE IS A FELONY CHARGE.

THE ARRAIGNMENT

THE VICTIM OF THE CRIME WILL BE NOTIFIED WHEN THE DEFENDANT IS ARRESTED AND TAKEN INTO POLICE CUSTODY. THE GOVERNMENT OFFICIALS MUST NOTIFY THE VICTIM OF THE DATE, TIME AND PLACE OF THE INITIAL APPEARANCE OF THE DEFENDANT IN COURT. THE VICTIM HAS THE RIGHT TO APPEAR AT THE ARRAIGNMENT AND WATCH THE PROCEEDINGS. HOWEVER. THE VICTIM IS NOT REQUIRED TO MAKE AN APPEARANCE AT THE INITIAL ARRAIGNMENT. THE DECISION TO APPEAR IS SOLEY WITHIN THE DISCRETION OF THE VICTIM OF THE CRIME.

AT THE ARRAIGNMENT, ONE FACTOR THAT THE JUDGE MUST CONSIDER IS WHETHER TO RELEASE THE DEFENDANT ON BAIL PENDING THE NEXT COURT HEARING. WHILE THE SETTING OF AN APPEARANCE BOND IS REQUIRED BY THE LAW, THE COURT, IN SETTING BOND, WILL CONSIDER THE FOLLOWING FACTORS:

1. THE NUMBER OF CHARGES THAT HAVE BEEN FILED;
2. THE SERIOUSNESS OF EACH OF THE OFFENSES;
3. THE POSSIBLE PUNISHMENT THAT EACH CHARGE CARRIES;
4. THE PRIOR CRIMINAL RECORD OF THE ACCUSED;
5. THE POSSIBLE FLIGHT RISK OF THE DEFENDANT; AND
6. WHETHER THE DEFENDANT HAS FAILED TO SHOW FOR A COURT HEARING IN THE PAST;

ONE ISSUE THAT IS INCLUDED IN THE SETTING OF BAIL IS THAT THE DEFENDANT BE ORDERED NOT TO HAVE ANY CONTACT WITH THE VICTIM OF THE CRIME. THE PURPOSE OF THE INCLUSION OF THIS PROVISION IS TO PREVENT THE DEFENDANT FROM HARASSING OR TRYING TO INTIMIDATE THE VICTIM IN ANY MANNER FROM HAVING THE CASE HEARD IN COURT ON ITS MERITS. ANY ACTION BY THE ACCUSED IN ATTEMPTING TO CONTACT THE VICTIM WILL RESULT IN THE DEFENDANT'S BOND BEING REVOKED AND THE DEFENDANT PLACE BACK IN JAIL UNTIL THE NEXT COURT DATE. ANY VIOLATION OF THE ORDER BY THE DEFENDANT COULD ALSO BE THE BASIS OF A "CONTEMPT OF COURT" CHARGE BEING FILED AGAINST THE DEFENDANT.

THE PRELIMINARY HEARING

IN ALL FELONY CASES, THE LAW OF EACH STATE REQUIRES THAT A "SHOW CAUSE" OR PRELIMINARY HEARING BE HELD IN THE CASE. THE PURPOSE OF THE PRELIMINARY HEARING IS FOR THE GOVERNMENT TO SHOW TWO THINGS:

FIRST, THAT A CRIME HAS BEEN COMMITTED AS ALLEGED IN THE COMPLAINT OR INDICTMENT. THE BURDEN OF PROOF IS ON THE GOVERNMENT TO PROVE THE COMMISSION OF THE CRIME BEYOND ANY REASONABLE DOUBT.

SECOND, THE GOVERNMENT MUST OFFER EVIDENCE THAT THE ACCUSED DEFENDANT HAS SOME CONNECTION TO THE CRIMINAL ACT. THE BURDEN OF PROOF BY THE GOVERNMENT ON THE SECOND ISSUE IS "BY A PREPONDERANCE OF THE EVIDENCE". THAT TERM MEANS THERE IS A LIKELY CONNECTION BETWEEN THE CRIME THAT HAS BEEN COMMITTED AND THE DEFENDANT.

THE VICTIM OF THE CRIME WILL BE NOTIFIED OF THE DATE, TIME AND PLACE OF THE PRELIMINARY HEARING BY THE PROSECUTOR'S OFFICE. APPROXIMATELY, TEN TO FOURTEEN DAYS PRIOR TO THE DATE OF THE HEARING, THE VICTIM WILL BE SERVED WITH A SUBPOENA (AN ORDER TO APPEAR AND TESTIFY). THE VICTIM MUST APPEAR WHEN SERVED WITH THE ORDER. FAILURE TO APPEAR COULD RESULT IN THE CASE BEING DISMISSED AND THE VICTIM BEING CITED FOR CONTEMPT OF COURT.

(PRELIMINARY HEARING-CONTINUED):

THE PROSECUTOR'S OFFICE WILL CONTACT THE VICTIM TO ARRANGE FOR THE VICTIM TO APPEAR AT HIS OFFICE 60 TO 90 MINUTES PRIOR TO THE START OF THE COURT HEARING IN ORDER TO PREPARE FOR THE COURT HEARING. DURING THIS MEETING, THE VICTIM WILL BE ALLOWED TO REVIEW ALL COURT FILINGS IN THE CASE AND THEIR STATEMENT GIVEN TO THE POLICE AT THE TIME THAT THE CRIME OCCURRED. THIS REVIEW ALLOWS THE VICTIM TO REFRESH THEIR MEMORY AND PREPARE FOR THEIR TESTIMONY IN COURT. THE PROSECUTING ATTORNEY WILL REVIEW THE QUESTIONS THAT HE WILL ASK THE VICTIME/WITNESS DURING THE COURT HEARING. THE PROSECUTOR WILL ALSO COVER THE QUESTIONS THAT THE VICTIM MAY BE ASKED BY DEFENSE COUNSEL DURING THE CROSS-EXAMINATION OF THE WITNESS. THE VICTIM MUST BE PREPARED IN ORDER TO OFFER THE PROPER TESTIMONY THAT THE COURT MUST CONSIDER IN ORDER TO HAVE THE DEFENDANT BOUND OVER FOR TRIAL. THE VICTIM MUST BE MENTALLY PREPARED TO FACE THE DEFENDANT IN THE COURTROOM. THE VICTIM WILL BE ASSURED BY THE PROSECUTOR THAT THE VICTIM HAS NOTHING TO FEAR DURING THE COURT HEARING. ONCE THE HEARING STARTS, THE VICTUM WILL BE PLACED IN A PRIVATE ROOM FOR WITNESSES (THE RULE OF SEQUESTRATION) UNTIL THE VICTIM IS CALLED INTO THE COURTROOM TO PRESENT THEIR TESTIMONY. ONCE THE VICTIM COMPLETES THEIR TESTIMONY, THEY ARE EXCUSED AND MAY LEAVE THE COURT PROCEEDINGS.

BIND-OVER ORDER

ONCE THE PRELIMINARY HEARING IS CONCLUDED, THE COURT WILL ANNOUNCE

A DECISION ON WHETHER THE DEFENDANT SHOULD BE BOUND OVER FOR TRIAL.

THE JUDGE, CONDUCTING THE HEARING, MUST FIND TWO FINDINGS OF FACT IN

ORDER TO ISSUE THE "BIND-OVER ORDER". THESE INCLUDE FINDING:

1. THAT THERE IS CREDIBLE EVIDENCE SHOWN TO THE COURT THAT
   A CRIME HAS BEEN COMMITTED IN THE JURISDICTION OF THE COURT.
   THIS EVIDENCE MUST BE SHOWN BEYOND A REASONABLE DOUBT;

2. THAT THE DEFENDANT HAS SOME CONNECTION TO THE CRIME THAT
   HAS BEEN COMMITTED. THIS EVIDENCE MUST BE SHOWN BY THE
   STANDARD IDENTIFIED AS A "PREPONDERANCE OF THE EVIDENCE".

ONCE THE JUDGE HAS MADE THAT FINDING IN THE RECORD, THE JUDGE

WILL ISSSUE THE ORDER, BINDING THE DEFENDANT OVER FOR TRIAL. A

PART OF THE BIND OVER ORDER REQUIRES THE DEFENDANT TO APPEAR

BEFORE THE ASSIGNED TRIAL JUDGE WITHIN 30 DAYS FOR HIS PRETRIAL

ARRAIGNMENT. THE JUDGE WILL ALSO ISSUE, AS A PART OF THE BIND OVER

ORDER, THE NEW ORDER ON THE BOND OR BAIL THAT MUST BE POSTED BY

THE DEFENDANT TO REMAIN OUT OF JAIL UNTIL THE NEXT COURT HEARING.

THE JUDGE HAS THE DISCRETION TO RAISE THE DEFENDANT'S BOND IF THERE

IS A FINDING BY THE COURT THAT THE DEFENDANT HAS COMMITTED MORE

CRIMES SINCE THE CRIMES THAT ARE ALLEGED IN THE ORIGINAL COMPLAINT.

THE PRETRAIL ARRAIGNMENT

THE BIND OVER ORDER REQUIRES THE DEFENDANT TO APPEAR FOR A PRETRIAL ARRAIGNMENT BEFORE THE ASSIGNED TRIAL JUDGE WITHIN 30 DAYS. AT THE PRETRIAL ARRAIGNMENT, THE TRIAL JUDGE WILL TAKE THE FOLLOWING ACTIONS:

1. READ THE COMPLAINT AND INFORMATION TO THE DEFENDANT; THE DEFENDANT MUST ACKNOWLEDGE THAT HE UNDERSTANDS THE CHARGES THAT ARE BEING MADE AGAINST HIM;

2. THE JUDGE WILL DEMAND THAT THE DEFENDANT ENTER A PLEA OF GUILTY OR NOT GUILTY TO THE CHARGES. AT THIS POINT IN THE PROCEEDINGS THE JUDGE WILL GENERALLY NOT ACCEPT A GUILTY PLEA FROM THE DEFENDANT;

3. THE JUDGE WILL ASK THE DEFENDANT IF HE HAS AN ATTORNEY TO REPRESENT HIM AT THE TRIAL OF THE CASE; THE DEFENDANT MUST AFFIRMATIVELY STATE THAT HE HAS AN ATTORNEY TO REPRESENT HIM. IF THE DEFENDANT INDICATES TO THE JUDGE THAT HE CAN NOT AFFORD AN ATTORNEY, HE MAY ASK FOR THE COURT TO APPOINT HIM AN ATTORNEY;

4. IF THE DEFENDANT REQUESTS A COURT APPOINTED ATTORNEY, THE JUDGE WILL SCHEDULE A RULE 8 HEARING TO DETERMINE IF THE DEFENDANT QUALIFIES FOR A COURT APPOINTED ATTORNEY.

5. IF THERE IS NO ISSUE ON THE ATTORNEY QUESTION, THE JUDGE WILL REQUEST THE DEFENDANT TO INDICATE WHETHER THE COURT SHOULD SET THE CASE FOR A "JURY TRIAL" OR A "NON-JURY" TRIAL.

(PRETRIAL ARRAIGNMENT CONTINUED):

6. THE JUDGE WILL SET A NON-JURY TRIAL GENERALLY WITHIN 90 DAYS OF THE PRETRIAL ARRAIGNMENT;

7. THE JUDGE WILL SET A JURY TRIAL AT THE NEXT SCHEDULED JURY DOCKET WITHIN THE JURISDICTION, GENERALLY WITHIN 12 MONTHS OF THE PRETRIAL ARRAIGNMENT;

8. THE JUDGE WILL SET A DEADLINE FOR THE FILING OF PRETRIAL MOTIONS; (THESE MOTIONS MAY INCLUDE: A MOTION FOR A CHANGE OF VENUE; RECUSAL OF THE JUDGE; MOTION FOR THE DISCOVERY OF EVIDENCE THAT WILL BE OFFERED AT TRIAL; A MOTION TO SUPPRESS EVIDENCE IF THERE HAS A SEARCH AND SEIZURE IN THE CASE OR IF THERE HAS BEEN A CONFESSION BY THE DEFENDANT IN THE CASE; THE MOTIONS DEADLINE IS GENERALLY SET WITH 60 TO 90 DAYS AFTER THE PRETRIAL ARRAIGNMENT;

9. THE JUDGE WILL THEN SET A PREHEARING CONFERENCE PRIOR TO THE START OF THE TRIAL BEFORE THE JURY TRIAL BEGINS.

10. THE LAST ISSUE THAT THE JUDGE ADDRESSES AT THE PRETRIAL ARRAIGNMENT IS THE ISSUE OF BOND. THE JUDGE WILL REVIEW THE BOND THAT THE DEFENDANT HAS POSTED WITH THE COURT AND DETERMINES WHETHER THE BOND SHOULD BE RAISED. THE JUDGE HAS THE DISCRETION TO RAISE THE BOND TO A HIGHER AMOUNT IF THERE IS A POSSIBILITY THAT THE DEFENDANT POSES A "FLIGHT RISK" AND MAY NOT SHOW UP WHEN THE CASE COMES ON FOR TRIAL. AS A CONDITION OF THE BOND, THE JUDGE WILL REMIND THAT THE DEFENDANT NOT HAVE ANY CONTACT WITH THE VICTIM IN ANY WAY, SHAPE OR FORM. FAILURE TO COMPLY WITH THE ORDER COULD RESULT IN THE DEFENDANT'S BOND BEING REVOKED AND THE DEFENDANT PLACED BACK IN JAIL.

THE VICTIM IS NOT REQUIRED TO APPEAR AT THE PRETRIAL ARRAIGNMENT.

THE VICTIM HAS THE DISCRETION IN DECIDING WHETHER TO APPEAR AT THE

HEARING. MOST VICTIMS DO NOT WANT TO APPEAR AT SUCH A HEARING.

THE TRIAL

THE TRIAL FOR THE DEFENDANT CHARGED WITH THE CRIME IS SET ON THE NEXT AVAILABLE JURY DOCKET, GENERALLY 9 TO 12 MONTHS AFTER THE PRE-TRIAL ARRAIGNMENT. THE PROSECUTOR'S OFFICE WILL NOTIFY THE VICTIM OF THE CRIME WHEN THE SCHEDULED JURY TRIAL IS PLACED ON THE COURT'S CALENDAR. THE VICTIM WILL RECEIVE WRITTEN NOTICE FROM THE PROSECUTOR'S APPROXIMATELY 20 DAYS PRIOR TO THE START OF THE TRIAL DOCKET. THE VICTIM WILL BE SCHEDULED TO COME INTO THE PROSECUTOR'S OFFICE TO PREPARE FOR THE UPCOMING TRIAL. AT THE CONFERENCE, THE VICTIM WILL BE ASKED TO EXAMINE THE COURT FILE CONTENTS RELATIVE TO THE PRELIMINARY HEARING TRANSCRIPT TO REFRESH THEIR MEMORY ABOUT THEIR PREVIOUS TESTIMONY. THE VICTIM WILL ALSO BE ALLOWED TO EXAMINE PHYSICAL EVIDENCE REPORTS THAT HAVE BEEN RENDERED BY EXPERT WITNESSES THAT WILL TESTIFY FOR THE GOVERNMENT. THE VICTIM WILL BE REQUIRED TO PREPARE FOR THEIR ANTICIPATED TESTIMONY BY THE PROSECUTOR ASKING THEM QUESTIONS ABOUT ISSUES THAT WILL ARISE DURING THE TRIAL, INCLUDING QUESTIONS DURING CROSS-EXAMINATION BY THE COUNSEL FOR THE DEFENSE. THE VICTIM SHOULD BE FULLY PREPARED WHEN THE TRIAL DATE ROLLS AROUND. APPROXIMATELY 10 DAYS PRIOR TO THE START OF THE TRIAL DOCKET, THE VICTIM WILL BE SERVED WITH A WRITTEN SUBPOENA BY THE COURT. THE SUBPOENA WILL OFFICIALLY NOTIFY THE VICTIM OF THE TIME, DATE AND PLACE TO APPEAR FOR THE TRIAL HEARING.

THE TRIAL PROCESS

THE JURY PANEL, THAT IS GOING TO HEAR THE CASE, WILL BE SUMMONED
TO THE COURTHOUSE BY THE TRIAL JUDGE. THE JURY PANEL WILL CONSIST
OF FELLOW CITIZENS OF THE COMMUNITY THAT ARE REGISTERED TO VOTE
IN THE DISTRICT WHERE THE TRIAL IS LOCATED.

THE "VOIR DIRE" PROCESS

THE PROSPTIVE JURORS (TWELVE IN NUMBER) WILL BE CALLED TO THE
BENCH AND SEATED IN THE JURY BOX. THE PROSPECTIVE JURORS WILL BE
QUESTIONED IN DETAIL ABOUT THEIR ELIGIBILTY TO SERVE AS JURORS
IN THE CASE. THE JUDGE WILL START THE PROCESS AND THEN ALLOW THE
DISTRICT ATTORNEY AND THE DEFENSE COUNSEL TO HAVE THE OPPORTUNITY
TO DISCUSS ISSUES ABOUT THE CASE WITH THE PROSPECTIVE JURORS.

CHALLENGES FOR CAUSE

ONCE THE "VOIR DIRE" PROCESS IS COMPLETED, THE TRIAL JUDGE WILL
RECESS THE COURT HEARING FOR A FEW MINUTES. THE JUDGE WILL
CONFER WITH THE ATTORNEYS IN HIS CHAMBERS TO DETERMINE IF THERE
ARE ANY "CHALLENGES FOR CAUSE" TO REMOVE A PROSPECTIVE JUROR.
BOTH PARTIES ARE ALLOWED UNLIMITED CHALLENGES FOR CAUSE IN THE CASE.

PEREMPTORY CHALLENGES

EVERY STATE'S CRIMINAL CODE ALLOWS BOTH THE STATE AND THE DEFENSE TO EXERCISE "PEREMPTORY CHALLENGES" WITH REGARD TO PROSPECTIVE JURORS. THE "PEREMPTORY CHALLENGE PROCESS" ALLOWS EACH SIDE TO EXCUSE A CERTAIN NUMBER OF JURORS WITHOUT HAVING TO RECITE A SPECIFIC REASON. THE NUMBER OF PEREMPTORY CHALLENGES ALLOWED IN A CRIMINAL CASE VARIES FROM STATE TO STATE. IN MISDEMEANOR CASES, THE MAXIMUM NUMBER OF CHALLENGES IS NO MORE THAN THREE. IN FELONY CASES, THE MAXIMUM NUMBER IS GENERALLY NO MORE THAN SIX. IN DEATH PENALTY CASES, THE MAXIMUN NUMBER IS NO MORE THAN NINE CHALLENGES.

OPENING STATEMENT BY THE STATE

ONCE ALL THE CHALLENGES ARE EXHAUSTED, THE JUDGE SEATS THE JURY AND ALLOWS EACH SIDE TO MAKE AN "OPENING STATEMENT". THE PURPOSE OF THE OPENING STATEMENT IS TO ALLOW THE STATE'S ATTORNEY TO TELL THE JURY PANEL THE FACTS OF THE CASE AND DESCRIBE THE WITNESSES THAT THE STATE WILL CALL TO SUPPORT THE CHARGES AGAINST THE DEFENDANT, ASKING THE JURY TO FIND THE DEFENDANT GUILTY IN THE CASE.

DEFENSE OPENING STATEMENT

ONCE THE DISTRICT ATTORNEY HAS COMPLETED HIS OPENING STATEMENT TO THE JURY, THE DEFENSE COUNSEL IS ALLOWED TO MAKE AN OPENING STATEMENT TO THE JURY. THE DEFENSE COUNSEL MAY OFFER HIS VIEW OF THE EVIDENCE THAT HE ANTICIPATES THAT WILL BE PRESENTED TO THE JURY. THE DEFENSE COUNSEL ALSO HAS THE OPTION "TO RESERVE" HIS OPENING STATEMENT UNTIL AFTER THE PROSECUTOR HAS RESTED THE STATE'S CASE AGAINST THE DEFENDANT. THE TIMING OF THE DEFENSE COUNSEL'S OPENING STATEMENT RESTS SOLELY WITH THE DEFENSE COUNSEL.

THE PROSECUTION WITNESSES

THE GOVERNMENT'S ATTORNEY WILL CALL WITNESSES TO THE STAND TO SUPPORT THE CRIMINAL CHARGES THAT HAVE BEEN MADE AGAINST THE DEFENDANT. THE ORDER OF THE WITNESSES TO BE CALLED IS LEFT TO THE DISCRETION OF THE DISTRICT ATTORNEY. GENERALLY, THE FIRST WITNESS CALLED BY THE STATE WILL BE A UNIFORM POLICE OFFICER WHO ARRIVED AT THE SCENE OF THE CRIME AFTER THE VICTIM CALLED THE POLICE EMERGENCY HOTLINE NUMBER----911. THE OFFICER WILL DESCRIBE THE CRIME SCENE IN DETAIL AND INITIAL STATEMENTS MADE BY THE VICTIM IMMEDIATELY AFTER THE CRIME WAS COMMITTED. THE OFFICER WILL BE ALLOWED TO STATE HIS OPINION ABOUT THE VICTIM'S APPEARANCE AND PHYSICAL CONDITION IN THE MINUTES AFTER THE CRIME OCCURRED.

STATE'S WITNESSES

WHEN THE UNIFORMED OFFICER CONCLUDES HIS TESTIMONY, THE DISTRICT ATTORNEY IS ALLOWED TO CALL OTHER OFFICERS WHO MAY HAVE RESPONDED TO THE CRIME SCENE, INCLUDING CRIME SCENE TECHNICIANS WHO MAY HAVE COLLECTED PHYSICAL EVIDENCE FROM THE CRIME SCENE. THE STATE WILL GENERALLY OFFER "EXPERT WITNESS" TESTIMONY FROM FORENSIC EXPERTS SUCH AS FINGERPRINT ANALYSIS, BLOOD ANALYSIS OR DNA EVIDENCE. THESE EXPERT WITNESSES WILL PRESENT PHYSICAL EVIDENCE THAT LINKS THE ACCUSED DEFENDANT TO THE CRIME SCENE AND THE VICTIM OF THE CRIME. THE LAST WITNESS GENERALLY CALLED TO TESTIFY BY THE STATE IS THE VICTIM OF THE CRIME. WHY WOULD THE VICTIM BE THE LAST WITNESS? THE PROSECUTOR'S STRATEGY, IN CALLING THE VICTIM AS THE LAST WITNESS, IS TO GIVE THE JURY "A LASTING IMPRESSION" ABOUT THE SEVERITY OF THE CRIME AND THE IMPACT THAT THE CRIME HAS HAD ON THE VICTIM. THE TESTIMONY OF THE VICTIM, ESPECIALLY IN PERSONAL CRIMES, IS A VERY POWERFUL TOOL IN CONVINCING THE JURY THAT THE DEFENDANT IS GUILTY BEYOND ANY REASONABLE DOUBT. THE APPEARANCE, DEMEANOR AND CREDIBILITY OF THE VICTIM IS CRUCIAL TO THE STATE BEING ABLE TO PERSUADE THE JURY TO DELIVER THE GUILTY VERDICT AGAINST THE DEFENDANT.

THE DEMURRER OF THE DEFENSE

WHEN THE GOVERNMENT IS FINISHED WITH THE PRESENTATION OF ITS EVIDENCE. THE PROSECUTOR WILL ADVISE THE COURT THAT THE STATE RESTS ITS CASE. AT THIS POINT IN THE TRIAL, THE DEFENSE COUNSEL WILL MAKE A "DEMURRER TO THE EVIDENCE". THE TERM "DEMURRER" MEANS THAT TAKING ALL THE EVIDENCE OFFERED BY THE GOVERNMENT AS TRUE, THERE IS STILL INSUFFICIENT EVIDENCE THAT A CRIME HAS BEEN COMMITED OR THAT THE DEFENDANT IS, IN ANY WAY, CONNECTED TO THE CRIME. THE JUDGE WILL GENERALLY TAKE A RECESS AND RETIRE TO THE JUDGE'S CHAMBERS TO CONSIDER THE MERITS OF THE MOTION. IN MOST CASES, THE JUDGE WILL RETURN TO OPEN COURT AND OVERRULE THE MOTION TO DISMISS AND ORDER THE CASE TO PROCEED.

EVIDENCE FOR THE DEFENSE

THE EVIDENCE PRESENTED BY THE DEFENSE IS DETERMINED BY THE DEFENSE COUNSEL. THE DEFENSE ATTORNEY WILL CALL WITNESSES WHO MAY HAVE BEEN AT THE CRIME SCENE AND THAT OFFER A DIFFERENT VIEW ON WHAT HAPPENED TO THE VICTIM. THESE WITNESSES MAY OFFER INFORMATION ABOUT THE CRIME SCENE, THE LIGHTING CONDITIONS OR OTHER INFORMATION THAT MAY CAST DOUBT ON THE VICTIM'S TESTIMONY. EXPERT WITNESSES MAY BE CALLED BY THE DEFENSE TO RAISE ISSUES ABOUT THE PHYSICAL EVIDENCE OBTAINED FROM THE CRIME SCENE.

DOES THE DEFENDANT TESTIFY?

THE BIG QUESTION FOR THE DEFENSE IS "DOES THE DEFENDANT TESTIFY"? THE FIFTH AMENDMENT PROTECTS A DFENDANT FROM HAVING TO TAKE THE WITNESS STAND TO TESTIFY IN HIS OWN DEFENSE. THE DEFENDANT HAS AN ABSOLUTE RIGHT TO "REMAIN SILENT" DURING THE ENTIRE TRIAL. THE DECISION OF WHETHER THE DEFENDANT SHOULD TESTIFY IS THE MOST CRUCIAL DECISION IN A CRIMINAL CASE. THE DEFENSE COUNSEL WILL CONSIDER SEVERAL FACTORS IN MAKING THAT DECISION. THESE FACTORS WILL GENERALLY INCLUDE THE FOLLOWING:

1. THE APPEARANCE AND THE DEMEANOR OF THE DEFENDANT; IN THIS REGARD, DOES THE DEFENDANT HAVE THE PROPER APPEARANCE AND ATTITUDE IN OFFERING HIS TESTIMONY?

2. DOES THE DEFENDANT HAVE A PRIOR RECORD OF CONVICTIONS FOR FELONY CRIMES? THE PRIOR CRIMINAL RECORD OF THE DEFENDANT CAN BE USED BY THE PROSECUTOR IN THE QUESTIONING OF THE DEFENDANT DURING CROSS-EXAMINATION;

3. WHAT IS THE STANDING OF THE DEFENDANT IN THE COMMUNITY? IS THE DEFENDANT A FAMILY MAN? WITH A WIFE & CHILDREN? A CHUCH MEMBER?

THE BIGGEST DECISION IN THE CASE IS DOES THE DEFENDANT TESTIFY?

REBUTTAL EVIDENCE

ONCE THE EVIDENCE AND TESTIMONY IS COMPLETED BY THE DEFENSE, THE GOVERNMENT HAS THE RIGHT TO PUT ON EVIDENCE IN REBUTTAL. THIS TYPE OF EVIDENCE IS ALLOWED TO REFUTE THE INFORMATION THAT HAS BEEN PUT ON BY THE DEFENSE. THE GOVERNMENT MAY CALL WITNESSES TO OFFER SOME EVIDENCE THAT MAY CONTRADICT WHAT DEFENSE PRESENTED IN ITS CASE IN CHIEF. THE REBUTTAL EVIDENCE IS LIMITED TO ONLY THOSE WITNESSES THAT OFFER NEW INFORMATION ABOUT THE CASE. ONCE THE GOVERNMENT HAS COMPLETED ITS REBUTTAL EVIDENCE, THE DEFENSE IS ALLOWED, UNDER THE LAW, TO PRESENT SUR-REBUTTAL EVIDENCE THAT MAY CONTRADICT WHAT THE GOVERNMENT HAS PRESENTED IN ITS REBUTTAL EVIDENCE. THE TRIAL JUDGE WILL RESTRICT SUCH EVIDENCE TO ONLY NEW EVIDENCE THAT ADDRESSES THE ISSUES RAISED IN THE STATE'S REBUTTLAL EVIDENCE.

JURY INSTRUCTIONS

ONCE ALL THE EVIDENCE HAS BEEN SUBMITTED BY BOTH THE GOVERNMENT AND THE DEFENSE, THE CASE IS READY TO BE SUBMITTED TO THE JURY FOR ITS DECISION. TO ASSIST THE JURY, THE TRIAL JUDGE IS REQUIRED TO ISSUE, ORALLY AND IN WRITING, INSTRUCTIONS ON THE LAW AND THE EVIDENCE TO GUIDE THE JURY IN THEIR DELIBERATIONS. WHILE EACH SIDE MAY SUBMIT REQUESTED JURY INSTRUCTIONS, THE JUDGE DECIDES WHICH ONES ARE GIVEN.

CLOSING ARGUMENTS

BOTH THE GOVERNMENT AND THE DEFENSE ARE ALLOWED TO MAKE CLOSING ARGUMENTS IN THE CASE. THE PURPOSE OF THE CLOSING ARGUMENTS IS TO ALLOW EACH SIDE TO SUMMARIZE THEIR POSITIONS IN THE CASE. SINCE THE STATE HAS THE BURDEN OF PROOF, THE STATE PROSECUTOR GOES FIRST IN THE CLOSING ARGUMENT PROCESS. THE PROSECUTION WILL REVIEW THE CRIMINAL CHARGES THAT HAVE BEEN FILED AGAINST THE DEFENDANT AND REVIEW THE TESTIMONY OF THE WITNESSES THAT HAVE BEEN CALLED TO SUPPORT THE STATE'S CASE. THE PROSECUTOR WILL EMPHASIZE THE TESTIMONY OF THE VICTIM OF THE CRIME AND THE IMPACT THAT THE CRIME HAS HAD ON THE VICTIM. AFTER THE PROSECUTOR HAS FINISHED THE FIRST PART OF HIS CLOSING ARGUMENT. THE DEFENSE IS ALLOWED TO PRESENT ITS CLOSING STATEMENT. DURING THE DEFENSE CLOSING ARGUMENT, THE DEFENSE COUNSEL WILL PLACE EMPHASIS ON THE WEAKNESSES IN THE GOVERNMENT'S CASE. THE DEFENSE WILL CONTEND THAT THE "BURDEN OF PROOF" IS ON THE STATE TO PROVE THE ELEMENTS OF THE CRIME BEYOND A REASONABLE DOUBT. ONCE THE DEFENSE IS FINISHED WITH ITS CLOSING ARGUMENT, THE GOVERNMENT IS ALLOWED TO MAKE ITS LAST ARGUMENT, APPEALING TO THE JURY TO CONVICT THE DEFENDANT BASED ON THE EVIDENCE AND DELIVER A VERDICT THAT WILL ADEQUATELY PUNISH THE DEFENDANT FOR THE CRIME. THE VICTIM IS ALLOWED TO SIT IN THE COURTROOM AND LISTEN TO BOTH STATE AND DEFENSE CLOSING ARGUMENTS

JURY DELIBERATIONS

WHEN THE PARTIES CONCLUDE THEIR RESPECTIVE CLOSING ARGUMENTS, THE CASE IS SUBMITTED TO THE JURY FOR THEIR DELIBERATIONS AND VERDICT. THE JUDGE WILL REMIND THE JURORS OF THEIR OATH TAKEN AS JURORS AND THEN DIRECT THE JURY MEMBERS TO RETIRE TO THE JURY ROOM TO BEGIN THEIR DELIBERATIONS. THE JURY WILL BE PLACED IN THE CUSTODY AND CARE OF THE COURT BAILIFF AND RETIRE TO THE JURY ROOM. THE RESPONSIBILITY OF THE BAILIFF IS TO ASSURE THE COURT THAT THE JURY IS SEQUESTORED IN THE JURY ROOM DURING THEIR DELIBERATIONS AND NOT SUBJECT TO ANY CONTACT WITH ANY OUTSIDE INDIVIDUALS OR THE NEWS MEDIA. WHAT GOES ON INSIDE THE JURY ROOM DURING JURY DELIBERATIONS? THE TRIAL JUDGE WILL ALLOW THE JURY TO TAKE ALL PHYSICAL EXHIBITS, THAT HAVE BEEN PROPERLY ADMITTED INTO EVIDENCE, INTO THE JURY ROOM. THESE EXHIBITS MAY INCLUDE THE FOLLOWING ITEMS:

1. PHOTOS OF THE CRIME SCENE;
2. PHOTOS OF THE VICTIM;
3. PHOTOS OF THE DEFENDANT;
4. MEDICAL RECORDS OF THE VICTIM;
5. PRIOR CRIMINAL RECORD OF THE ACCUSED;
6. VIDEO TAPED STATEMENTS (A CONFESSION) MADE BY THE DEFENDANT AT THE POLICE STATION FOLLOWING HIS ARREST.

THE JURY VERDICT

THE FIRST ITEM OF BUSINESS THAT THE JURY MUST DECIDE IN THE JURY ROOM IS THE SELECTION OF ONE PERSON TO SERVE AS FOREMAN OR SPOKEPERSON FOR THE JURY. THE JOB OF THE FOREMAN IS TO LEAD THE JURY IN THEIR REVIEW AND ANALYSIS OF ALL THE EVIDENCE, TESTIMONY AND PHYSICAL EXHIBITS THAT HAVE BEEN ADMITTED INTO EVIDENCE. JURY DELIBERATIONS MAY CONTINUE FOR SEVERAL HOURS OR DAYS AFTER THE CASE HAS BEEN SUBMITTED. THERE IS "NO TIME LIMIT" PLACED ON THE JURY BY THE JUDGE IN CONDUCTING THEIR DELIBERATIONS. ANY VERDICT THAT THE JURY RENDERS MUST BE UNANIMOUS; (THAT IS ALL 12 MEMBERS OF THE JURY MUST AGREE ON THE DEFENDANT'S GUILT OR INNOCENCE). ONCE THE JURY HAS REACHED A VERDICT, THE FOREMAN OF THE JURY MUST SIGN THE JURY VERDICT FORM. IN THE EVENT THAT THE JURY VERDICT IS A FINDING OF GUILT ON THE PART OF THE DEFENDANT, THE JURY MUST CONSIDER AND RECOMMEND A PROPER PUNISHMENT FOR THE DEFENDANT. IN THE EVENT THAT THE JURY IS UNABLE TO REACH A UNANIMOUS VERDICT (THE JURY IS SPLIT BETWEEN "GUILTY OR NOT GUILTY"), THE FOREMAN MUST NOTIFY THE BAILIFF OF THE JURY DEADLOCK. THE JUDGE WILL ORDER THE JURY TO RETURN TO THE COURTROOM. THE JUDGE MAY ACCEPT THE "GUILTY" OR "NOT GUILTY" VERDICT. IF THE JURY IS DEADLOCKED, THE JUDGE WILL DISCHARGE THE JURY AND RESET THE CASE FOR ANOTHER DIFFERENT JURY PANEL AT A LATER DATE.

READING THE VERDICT

ONCE THE JURY RETURNS TO OPEN COURT, THE VERDICT FORMS ARE DELIVERED TO THE JUDGE. THE JUDGE READS THE VERDICT FORMS SILENTLY AND DETERMINES WHETHER THE VERDICT IS ACCEPTABLE. THE JUDGE WILL THEN HAND THE VERDICT FORMS TO THE CLERK TO BE READ ALOUD IN OPEN COURT. AFTER THE READING OF THE VERDICT, THE JUDGE WILL INQUIRE OF THE MEMBERS OF THE JURY WHETHER THE VERDICT FORM REPRESENTS THEIR DECISION IN THE CASE. THE JUDGE WILL ALLOW BOTH THE PROSECUTOR AND THE DEFENSE COUNSEL TO EXAMINE THE VERDICT FORM FOR ANY POSSIBLE IRREGULARITIES. BOTH ATTORNEYS MUST AFFIRMATIVELY STATE THAT THE VERDICT FORM IS PROPERLY EXECUTED BY THE MEMBERS OF THE JURY. ANY OBJECTIONS BY COUNSEL MUST BE CLEARLY STATED INTO THE RECORD BEING TAKEN IN THE CASE BY THE COURT REPORTER. THE JUDGE WILL THEN DIRECT THE CLERK TO FILE THE VERDICT IN THE COURT FILE. THE JUDGE WILL THEN THANK THE JURY FOR THEIR SERVICE AND DISCHARGE THEM. THE WORK OF THE JURY IS COMPLETE. JURY MEMBERS ARE ESCORTED FROM THE COURTROOM BY THE BAILIFF AND TAKEN TO THE COURT CLERK'S OFFICE TO SIGN PAPERWORK RELATED TO THEIR JURY SERVICE. IN A FEW WEEKS, THE MEMBERS OF THE JURY WILL RECEIVE A "TOKEN PAYMENT" FROM THE COURT FOR THEIR SERVICES RENDERED IN THE CASE.

POST TRIAL ISSUES

AFTER THE JURY IS DISCHARGED FROM THE COURTROOM, THE JUDGE WILL MAKE A STATEMENT INTO THE RECORD. IN THE EVENT THAT THE DEFENDANT HAS BEEN FOUND "NOT GUILTY", THE JUDGE WILL ORDER THE DEFENDANT BE RELEASED FROM CUSTODY AND THE BOND POSTED BE EXONERATED. IN THE EVENT THAT THE DEFENDANT IS FOUND GUILTY, THE JUDGE WILL THEN SET A DATE FOR JUDGMENT AND SENTENCING OF THE DEFENDANT. THE DEFENSE COUNSEL WILL GENERALLY FILE SEVERAL POST TRIAL MOTIONS. THESE MOTIONS MAY INCLUDE THE FOLLOWING:

1. MOTION FOR A COURT JUDGMENT FINDING THE DEFENDANT NOT GUILTY NOT WITHSTANDING THE FINDING OF GUILT BY THE JURY. IN A LARGE MAJORITY OF THESE CASES, THE JUDGE WILL SUMMARILY OVERRULE THIS MOTION. JUDGES ARE VERY RELUCTANT TO SET ASIDE A VERDICT RENDERED BY JURY COMPOSED OF PEOPLE IN THE SURROUNDING COMMUNITY.
2. MOTION FOR NEW TRIAL. THE DEFENSE COUNSEL MAY SEEK A NEW TRIAL, BASED ON THE GROUNDS THAT THE JURY VERDICT WAS BASED ON IMPROPER EVIDENCE, PROSECUTOR MISCONDUCT, IMPROPER INSTRUCTIONS GIVEN TO THE JURY BY THE COURT OR OTHER GROUNDS THAT DEPRIVED THE DEFENDANT TO A FAIR TRIAL UNDER THE 6TH AMENDMENT OF THE CONSTITUTION.
3. DEFENSE COUNSEL'S REQUEST FOR A "PRESENTENCE INVESTIGATION BY THE COURT" TO DETERMINE IF THE DEFENDANT IS ENTITLED TO PROBATION SENTENCE.

PRESENTENCE REPORT

THE JUDGE WILL ORDER A "PRESENTENCE INVESTIGATION" AT THE REQUEST OF THE DEFENDANT OR THE GOVERNMENT. THE PROBATION AND PAROLE DIVISION OF THE STATE'S DEPARTMENT OF CORRECTIONS WILL ASSIGN A PAROLE OFFICER TO DO THE INVESTIGATION AND REPORT. THE PURPOSE OF THE PRESENTENCE INVESTIGATION IS GIVE THE COURT A COMPREHENSIVE BACKGROUND REPORT ON THE CONVICTED DEFENDANT'S PAST CHARACTER, EMPLOYMENT HISTORY, FAMILY AND PRIOR RECORD WITH THE CRIMINAL JUSTICE SYSTEM. THE INVESTIGATING OFFICER WILL TYPICALLY REVIEW THE COURT FILE; TAKE STATEMENTS FROM THE VICTIM AND POLICE OFFICERS; AND DO A COMPREHENSIVE REVIEW OF THE DEFENDANT PRIOR CRIMINAL CONVICTIONS. THE VICTIM OF THE CRIME WILL BE ALLOWED TO PRESENT INFORMATION RELATIVE TO THE IMPACT OF THE CRIME ON THE VICTIM'S LIFE. ONCE THE INVESTIGATION IS COMPLETED, THE PAROLE OFFICER WILL PREPARE AND FORWARD HIS REPORT TO THE COURT ALONG WITH THE OFFICER'S RECOMMENDATIONS AS TO THE NATURE AND EXTENT OF THE SENTENCE THAT SHOULD BE IMPOSED BY THE COURT ON THE CONVICTED DEFENDANT. THE PRESENTENCE INVESTIGATION TYPICALLY TAKE SIX TO EIGHT WEEKS TO COMPLETE. THE ORIGINAL REPORT IS FORWARDED TO THE COURT CLERK WITH A COPY FURNISHED TO THE STATE'S ATTORNEY AND THE DEFENSE COUNSEL.

JUDGMENT AND SENTENCING

THE COURT HEARING ON THE JUDGMENT AND SENTENCING OF THE DEFENDANT WILL GENERALLY BE SET APPROXIMATELY 60 DAYS AFTER THE JURY VERDICT IS FILED IN THE CASE. THE PENAL CODES OF MOST STATES REQUIRE THAT THE STATE FURNISH A COPY OF THE PRESENTENCE REPORT TO THE VICTIM(S) OF THE CRIME PRIOR TO THE COURT DATE SET FOR DISPOSITION OF THE CASE. THE VICTIM OF THE CRIME HAS THE RIGHT TO APPEAR AT THE JUDGMENT AND SENTENCING HEARING. MOST STATE ALLOW THE VICTIM TO PREPARE AND FURNISH TO THE COURT AND COUNSEL A "VICTIM'S IMPACT STATEMENT. THE CONTENTS OF "THE VICTIM'S IMPACT STATEMENT" VARIES FROM STATE TO STATE. THE VICTIM MAY READ THE READ THE STATEMENT TO THE COURT AND HAVE THE STATEMENT MADE A PART OF THE OFFICIAL RECORD IN THE CASE. THE VICTIM'S PERSONAL IMPACT STATEMENT WILL GENERALLY INCLUDE THE FOLLOWING:

1. A COMPLETE DESCRIPTION OF THE PERSONAL INJURIES SUSTAINED BY THE VICTIM AS A RESULT OF THE CRIME;
2. AN ITEMIZED LIST OF THE MEDICAL EXPENSES INCURRED;
3. A DESCRIPTION OF THE PHYSICAL PROPERTY DAMAGE SUSTAINED BY THE VICTIM;
4. A ITEMIZATION OF THE LOST WAGES AND TIME LOST FROM WORK DUE TO THE CRIME OR APPEARING FOR COURT TO TESTIFY IN THE COURT PROCEEDINGS;
5. THE EMOTIONAL IMPACT THE CRIME HAS HAD ON THE VICTIM'S LIFE;
6. THE VICTIM'S RECOMMENDATION ON THE DEFENDANT'S PUNISHMENT.

-26-

THE SENTENCE OF THE COURT

THE JUDGE, DURING OF THE HEARING, WILL ALLOW THE GOVERNMENT'S

ATTORNEY AND THE DEFENSE COUNSEL TO ADDRESS THE COURT WITH

REGARD TO THE PRESENTENCE REPORT, THE JURY VERDICT AND THE

VICTIM'S IMPACT STATEMENT. EACH SIDE WILL BE ALLOWED TO PRESENT

ARGUMENTS ON WHAT THE JUDGE SHOULD DO WITH REGARD TO THE

SENTENCE TO BE IMPOSED ON THE DEFENDANT. THE DEFENDANT WILL

BE ALLOWED TO ADDRESS THE COURT AND MAKE A PLEA FOR "LENIENCY".

THE JUDGE, AFTER CONSIDERING ALL OF THESE FACTORS, WILL ASK

THE COUNSEL TO STAND AND HEAR THE JUDGE IMPOSE THE COURT'S

SENTENCE ON THE DEFENDANT. THE JUDGE WILL ADVISE THE DEFENDANT

OF HIS RIGHT TO APPEAL HIS SENTENCE TO THE CRIMINAL COURT OF

APPEALS. THE JUDGE WILL ADVISE THE DEFENDANT THAT THE APPEAL

MUST BE FILED IN A TIMELY FASHION (GENERALLY WITHIN 30 TO 60 DAYS)

AFTER THE SENTENCE OF THE COURT. THE FINAL ITEM THAT THE JUDGE

WILL CONSIDER IS THE AMOUNT OF THE APPEAL BOND THAT SHOULD BE

SET DURING THE APPEAL PROCESS. THE AMOUNT OF THE APPEAL BOND

WILL DEPEND ON SEVERAL FACTORS, INCLUDING THE SEVERITY OF THE

CRIME(S); THE SENTENCE IMPOSED BY THE COURT; AND THE POSSIBLE

FLIGHT RISK IF THE DEFENDANT IS ALLOWED TO REMAIN FREE ON BOND

DURING THE APPEAL WHICH COULD TAKE 3 TO 5 YEARS TO BE HEARD.

THE DEFENDANT MAY BE RELEASED FROM CUSTODY WHEN THE BAIL IS

POSTED WITH THE CLERK OF THE COURT WHERE THE TRIAL WAS CONDUCTED.

THE CRIMINAL APPEAL

EVERY DEFENDANT CONVICTED IN A CRIMINAL CASE IN THE UNITED STATES CRIMINAL JUSTICE SYSTEM HAS THE RIGHT TO APPEAL HIS CONVICTION TO AN APPELLATE COURT. IN A FEDERAL COURT CASE, THE DEFENDANT HAS A RIGHT OF APPEAL TO THE FEDERAL COURT OF APPEALS IN THAT AREA. IN STATE CASES, THE DEFENDANT HAS THE RIGHT TO APPEAL TO THAT STATE'S COURT OF CRIMINAL APPEALS. EVERY STATE HAS SPECIFIC LAWS ON THE PROCESS FOR A CRIMINAL APPEAL. THE FIRST DOCUMENT FILED IN A CRIMINAL APPEAL IS THE "PETITION FOR REVIEW". THE PAPERWORK MUST BE FILED WITHIN A SPECIFIC TIME DEADLINE, GENERALLY WITHIN 30 TO 60 DAYS AFTER THE DATE OF THE JUDGMENT AND SENTENCING BY THE TRIAL COURT. THE APPEAL MUST INCLUDE A "DESIGNATION OF THE RECORD" OF THE TRIAL COURT PROCEEDINGS. THE COURT REPORTER, OF THE TRIAL COURT, MUST COMPLETE THE TRANSCRIPT OF ALL THE COURT PROCEEDINGS IN THE TRIAL COURT INCLUDING THE TESTIMONY OF THE WITNESSES, THE STATEMENTS OF THE PROSECUTOR AND THE DEFENSE COUNSEL. THE PREPARATION OF THE TRIAL RECORD GENERALLY TAKES A MINIMUM OF SIX MONTHS TO COMPLETE AND FORWARD TO THE APPELLATE COURT. THE TRIAL COURT CLERK MUST PREPARE AND FURNISH TO THE APPELLATE COURT ALL DOCUMENTS FILED IN THE CASE, INCLUDING THE ORDERS AND JURY INSTRUCTIONS GIVEN BY THE TRIAL JUDGE TO THE JURY IN THE CASE.

THE APPELLATE PROCESS

ONCE ALL THE RECORDS OF THE TRIAL COURT HAS BEEN FILED WITH THE APPELLATE COURT, THE APPEALS COURT WILL NOTIFY THE PARTIES BY FILING A "COMPLETION OF RECORD" NOTIFICATION IN THE CASE. ONCE THE COMPLETION OF RECORD IS FILED IN THE CASE, THE DEFENDANT WILL HAVE SIXTY DAYS TO FILE HIS APPEAL BRIEF, OUTLINING ALL THE ISSUES AND ERRORS MADE BY THE TRIAL COURT THAT RESULTED IN HIS CONVICTION. AN EXTENSION OF 20 TO 30 DAYS TO FILE THE DEFENDANT'S APPEAL BRIEF MAY BE GRANTED IN SOME CASES. ONCE THE DEFENSE APPEAL BRIEF HAS BEEN FILED WITH THE APPELLATE COURT, THE STATE'S ATTORNEY WILL HAVE 30 DAYS TO FILE A RESPONSE BRIEF, PRESENTING LEGAL JUSTIFICTION FOR THE APPELLATE COURT TO DENY THE DEFENDANT'S APPEAL. AT THIS POINT IN THE APPELLATE PROCESS, THE CASE STANDS SUBMITTED FOR THE COURT'S DECISION. THE APPELLATE COURT MAY TAKE SEVERAL MONTHS OR YEARS TO REVIEW THE TRIAL RECORDS AND APPEAL BRIEFS. IN SELECTED CASES, THE APPELLATE COURT MAY REQUEST THE ATTORNEYS REPRESENTING BOTH SIDES TO APPEAR BEFORE THE COURT TO PRESENT "ORAL ARGUMENTS". DURING THE "ORAL ARGUMENTS" HEARING, BOTH SIDES WILL BE ALLOWED UP TO ONE HOUR TO MAKE THEIR RESPECTIVE ARGUMENTS TO THE HIGH COURT ON THE DISPOSITION OF THE CASE. THE "ORAL ARGUMENTS" HEARING IS OPEN TO THE PUBLIC. THE VICTIM OF THE CRIME MAY ATTEND THE HEARING AND LISTEN TO THE PROCESS BUT THE VICTIM WILL NOT BE ALLOWED TO SPEAK DURING THE "ORAL ARGUMENTS" HEARING.

THE COURT DECISION

THE APPELLATE COURT DECISION WILL BE HANDED DOWN BY WRITTEN OPINION GENERALLY WITHIN 12 MONTHS AFTER THE ORAL ARGUMENTS ARE PRESENTED IN THE CASE. THE APPELLATE COURT HAS THREE OPTIONS IN RENDERING ITS FINAL DECISION. THESE OPTIONS ARE AS FOLLOWS:

1. AFFIRM THE CONVICTION OF THE DEFENDANT AND DENY HIS APPEAL;
2. AFFIRM THE CONVICTION BUT MODIFY THE PUNISHMENT ASSESSED BY THE TRIAL COURT DUE TO AN ERROR OF THE JUDGE DURING THE TRIAL OF THE CASE;
3. REVERSE THE DEFENDANT'S CONVICTION AND REMAND THE CASE BACK TO THE TRIAL COURT FOR A NEW TRIAL OR OTHER DISPOSITION OF THE CASE.

ONCE THE DECISION OF THE APPELLATE COURT HAS BEEN ISSUED, BOTH PARTIES MAY PETITION THE COURT FOR A REHEARING. THE PETITION FOR REHEARING MUST BE FILED IN A TIMELY MANNER, WITHIN 20 TO 30 DAYS AFTER THE OPINION IS RENDERED. THE APPELLATE COURT WILL REVIEW THE PETITION FOR REHEARING AND ISSUE AN OPINION WITH 30 TO 60 DAYS. IN THE EVENT THAT THE DEFENDANT'S CONVICTION IS AFFIRMED BY THE APPELLATE COURT, THE DEFENDANT HAS THE RIGHT TO FILE A "DIRECT APPEAL" TO THE U.S. SUPREME COURT. MOST DIRECT APPEALS TO THE U.S. SUPREME COURT ARE SUMMARILY DENIED BY THE HIGH COURT.

WRIT OF HABEUS CORPUS

WHEN THE FINAL STATE APPEAL IS DENIED, THE DEFENDANT IS REQUIRED TO APPEAR BEFORE THE TRIAL COURT WHERE THE FINAL SENTENCE WILL BE IMPOSED AND THE CONVICTED DEFENDANT BE ORDERED TO SURRENDER AND BEGIN SERVING HIS TERM OF CONFINEMENT IN THE STATE'S PRISON SYSTEM. ONCE THE DEFENDANT IS IN THE CUSTODY OF A STATE'S PRISON SYSTEM, THE CONVICTED DEFENDANT HAS AN INHERENT RIGHT TO CHALLENGE THE LEGALITY OF HIS CONFINEMENT UNDER THE BILL OF RIGHTS OF THE UNITED STATES CONSTITUTION. THE PROCESS OF CHALLENGING THE CONFINEMENT IS IDENTIFIED AS A "WRIT OF HABEUS CORPUS" PROCEEDING. THE "WRIT OF HABEUS CORPUS" PROCEEDING IS A CIVIL ACTION THAT IS FILED IN THE FEDERAL DISTRICT COURT WHERE THE DEFENDANT IS CONFINED TO PRISON. THE ACTION IS FILED AGAINST THE WARDEN OF THE PRISON THAT HAS PHYSICAL CUSTODY OF THE DEFENDANT. THE DEFENDANT (WARDEN) MUST FILE A WRITTEN RESPONSE TO THE CIVIL ACTION WITHIN 30 DAYS. THE FEDERAL DISTRICT JUDGE ASSIGNED TO THE CASE WILL ORDER THAT AN "EVIDENTIARY HEARING" BE HELD BEFORE THE COURT TO HEAR ANY WITNESSES THAT MAY OFFER TESTIMONY TO SUPPORT THE DEFENDANT'S CLAIM OF AN ILLEGAL CONFINEMENT. THE FEDERAL TRIAL COURT WILL RENDER ITS DECISION WITHIN SIX MONTHS. THE FEDERAL MAY GRANT THE WRIT AND ORDER THE RELEASE OF THE INMATE IF THERE IS EVIDENCE TO SUPPORT THE CLAIM THAT THE DEFENDANT'S RIGHTS WERE VIOLATED.

THE SUPREME COURT REVIEW

THE SUPREME COURT, UNDER ARTICLE III OF THE CONSTITUTION, HAS THE FINAL AUTHORITY TO DETERMINE THE VALIDITY OF A "WRIT OF HABEUS CORPUS" CLAIM. THE SUPREME COURT RECEIVES THOUSANDS OF REQUESTS EACH YEAR TO REVIEW APPEALS ON HABEUS CORPUS CASES. THE COURT, AS A RULE, WILL TYPICALLY DENY OVER 90% OF THE HABUES CORPUS APPEALS FROM LOWER FEDERAL COURTS. ONLY IN THOSE CASES, WHERE THERE IS A UNIQUE QUESTION OF CONSTITUTIONAL LAW, WILL THE COURT ACCEPT THE APPEAL AND REVIEW THE CASE. IF THE HIGH COURT ISSUES AN ORDER DENYING OF THE APPEAL, THE CONVICTION IS FINAL. THERE ARE NO FURTHER APPEALS IN THE AMERICAN CRIMINAL JUSTICE SYSTEM.

A PRESIDENTIAL PARDON

THE AMERICAN LEGAL SYSTEM ALLOWS THE PRESIDENT OF THE UNITED STATES TO ISSUE "A PARDON" TO A DEFENDANT CONVICTED IN UNITED STATES FEDERAL COURT OF COMMITTING A FEDERAL CRIME. THE LEGAL IMPACT OF A "PRESIDENTIAL PARDON" IS THAT THE CONVICTION OF THE DEFENDANT IS OVERTURNED AND THE DEFENDANT IS RELEASED FROM SERVING ANY TIME IN A CORRECTIONAL FACILITY.

A GOVERNOR'S PARDON

THE 10TH AMENDMENT OF THE UNITED STATES CONSTITUTION PROVIDES THAT CERTAIN POWERS ARE TO BE RESERVED TO EACH RESPECTIVE STATE. THE BASIC PURPOSE OF THE 10TH AMENDMENT IS TO ALLOW EACH OF THE FIFTY STATES TO ESTABLISH LAWS NECESSARY TO PRESERVE LAW AND ORDER IN THEIR STATE. EVERY STATE'S CONSTITUTION VESTS THE GOVERNOR OF THAT STATE WITH THE POWER TO ISSUE A "GOVERNOR'S PARDON" WITH REGARD TO A CONVICTION ISSUED BY A STATE'S CRIMINAL COURTS. A PARDON ISSUED BY THE GOVENOR OF THE STATE OVERTURNS THE CONVICTION OF THE DEFENDANT AND ORDERS THE STATE'S CORRECTIONS DEPARTMENT TO RELEASE THE DEFENDANT FROM CUSTODY.

VICTIM'S RIGHTS IN AMERICA

THE AMERICAN CRIMINAL JUSTICE SYSTEM, IN THE LAST SIXTY (60) YEARS, HAS PLACED THE MOST EMPHASIS ON THE RIGHTS OF THE DEFENDANT. THE WARREN COURT ERA (IN THE 1960'S AND 1970'S) HANDED DOWN KEY DECISIONS IN THE CASES LIKE MAPP V. OHIO (1961), GIDEON V. WAINWRIGHT (1963) AND MIRANDA V. ARIZONA (1966) WHICH RESULTED IN THE DEFENDANT'S CONVICTION BEING REVERSED AND THE CASE BEING REMANDED BACK TO STATE COURT FOR A RETRIAL OR A DISMISSAL OF THE CASE. THE WARREN COURT GAVE VERY LITTLE CONSIDERATION FOR THE PROTECTION OF THE RIGHTS OF THE VICTIMS IN THESE CASES. MANY STATES, (DURING THE 1980'S AND 1990'S), STARTED PASSING LAWS THAT WERE DESIGNED TO PROTECT A VICTIM'S RIGHTS AND SET UP VICTIM'S COMPENSATION PROGRAMS.

"THE U.S. JUSTICE FOR ALL ACT"(2004)

FEDERAL LAW GRANTS, THE VICTIM OF A VIOLENT CRIME, CERTAIN

STATUTORY RIGHTS, INCUDING THE FOLLOWING:

1. THE RIGHT TO BE PROTECTED FROM THE ACCUSED;
2. THE RIGHT TO BE TIMELY NOTIFIED OF ANY COURT
   PROCEEDING INVOLVING THE CRIME IN QUESTION
   OR THE ACCUSED;
3. THE RIGHT TO BE PRESENT AT ANY PUBLIC HEARING
   INVOLVING THE AJUDICATION, TRIAL HEARING, PLEA
   HEARING OR SENTENCING OF THE ACCUSED RELATED
   TO THE CRIME IN QUESTION;
4. THE RIGHT TO MEET AND CONFER WITH THE PROSECUTION
   OR GOVERNMENT'S ATTORNEY PRIOR TO ANY COURT
   HEARING INVOLVING THE ACCUSED OR THE VICTIM;
5. THE RIGHT TO RECEIVE, FROM THE ACCUSED, ANY AND
   ALL RESTITUTION AS PROVIDED BY LAW;
6. THE RIGHT TO A SPEEDY TRIAL OR DISPOSITION OF THE
   CRIMINAL CHARGES AGAINST THE ACCUSED;
7. THE RIGHT TO BE TREATED WITH FAIRNESS AND RESPECT
   BY THE GOVERNMENT'S ATTORNEY, THE COURT AND THE
   DEFENSE COUNSEL;
8. THE RIGHT TO PRIVACY DURING THE COURT ADJUDICATION
   OR DISPOSITION OF THE CASE;
9. THE RIGHT TO BE TIMELY INFORMED OF ANY PLEA BARGAIN,
   DEFERRED PROSECUTION, OR DEFERRED SENTENCE IN THE CASE
   THAT IS BEING CONSIDERED BY THE PROSECUTOR OR THE JUDGE.

THE HISTORY OF "VICTIM'S IMPACT STATEMENTS"

IN 1982, PRESIDENT RONALD REAGAN DIRECTED AN EXECUTIVE TASK FORCE TO EXAMINE ISSUES IN THE AMERICAN CRIMINAL JUSTICE SYSTEM AND MAKE RECOMMENDATIONS TO CONSIDER IN IMPROVING THE TREATMENT OF VICTIMS IN FEDERAL COURTS. ONE OF THE MANY RECOMMENDATIONS OF THE TASK FORCE WAS TO ALLOW "THE USE OF VICTIM IMPACT STATEMENTS" IN CRIMINAL TRIALS. THE ATTORNEY GENERAL'S OFFICE OF THE UNITED STATES GOVERNMENT ISSUED GUIDELINES FOR THE FEDERAL COURTS TO CONSIDER IN ALLOWING A "VICTIM'S IMPACT STATEMENT" INTO EVIDENCE. MOST STATES, THROUGH THEIR RESPECTIVE LEGISLATURES, ENACTED SIMILIAR LAWS TO ALLOW A VICTIM'S IMPACT STATEMENTS INTO EVIDENCE FOR A COURT TO CONSIDER IN IMPOSING A SENTENCE ON THE CONVICTED CRIMINAL. SEVERAL COURT CHALLENGES WERE MADE IN FEDERAL AND STATE COURTS. THE UNITED STATES SUPREME COURT (IN THE CASE OF PAYNE V. TENNESSEE , (1991) CONCLUDED THAT "VICTIM'S IMPACT STATEMENTS" WAS A PROPER PART OF THE EVIDENCE THAT THE COURT MAY CONSIDER IN IMPOSING A FINAL SENTENCE ON THE CONVICTED DEFENDANT. CURRENTLY, THERE ARE CURRENTLY 44 STATES THAT ALLOW "VICTIM'S IMPACT STATEMENTS" TO BE CONSIDERED BY THE COURTS.

VICTIM'S IMPACT STATEMENTS

WHAT IS "A VICTIM'S IMPACT STATEMENT"? A VICTIM'S IMPACT STATEMENT IS AN ORAL OR WRITTEN STATEMENT WHICH ALLOWS THE VICTIM OF A CRIME TO APPEAR BEFORE THE COURT (THE JUDGE) DURING THE SENTENCING PHASE OF THE CRIMINAL CASE AND PROVIDE INFORMATION TO THE COURT ON THE FOLLOWING ISSUES:

1. THE IMPACT OF THE CRIME ON THE VICTIM'S PERSONAL LIFE;
2. THE PHYSICAL INJURIES AND TRAUMA THAT THE VICTIM SUSTAINED AS A RESULT OF THE CRIME;
3. THE MEDICAL TREATMENT AND THERAPY RECEIVED BY THE VICTIM RESULTING FROM THE CRIME;
4. THE MEDICAL EXPENSES THAT THE VICTIM INCURRED AS A RESULT OF THE CRIME;
5. MENTAL HEALTH COUNSELING AND EXPENSES INCURRED BY THE VICTIM RELATED TO THE TRAUMA FROM THE CRIME;
6. A STATEMENT OF THE LOST TIME FROM WORK AND THE LOSS OF WAGES RESULTING FROM THE CRIME;
7. THE MEDICAL RECORDS OF THE VICTIM SUPPORTING THE FACTS INDICATED OF THE VICTIM'S IMPACT STATEMENT;

THE SUPPORTING DOCUMENTATION IS ESSENTIAL FOR THE COURT TO FULLY UNDERSTAND THE IMPACT OF THE CRIME ON THE VICTIM.

RESTITUTION

ONE OF THE FUNDAMENTAL PRINCIPLES OF THE AMERICAN CRIMINAL JUSTICE SYSTEM IS THAT THE DEFENDANT BE PROPERLY PUNISHED FOR HIS CRIME. THE MOST RECENT TREND OF THE CRIMINAL COURTS IN AMERICA IS "ORDERING RESTITUTION" AS A PART OF THE COURT ORDERED PUNSIHMENT. WHAT IS RESTITUTION? THE COURT ORDERS THE ACCUSED TO MAKE FINANCIAL PAYMENTS TO THE VICTIM FOR THE HARM CAUSED TO THE VICTIM. THE COURT MAY DIRECT THE DEFENDANT, AS A PART OF THE COURT'S JUDGMENT AND SENTENCING, TO PAY:

A. THE MEDICAL EXPENSES INCURRED BY THE
   VICTIM FOR TREATMENT OF INJURIES CAUSED
   BY THE CRIME;
B. LOST WAGES SUSTAINED BY THE VICTIM
   DUE TO LOST TIME FROM WORK;
C. LOST OF COMPENSATION DUE TO TIME MISSED
   FROM WORK WHILE ATTENDING COURT HEARINGS;
D. DAMAGES TO REAL OR PERSONAL PROPERTY
   CAUSED BY THE ACCUSED AT THE SCENE OF THE CRIME;
E. OTHER EXPENSES SUSTAINED BY THE VICTIM RESULTING
   FROM THE CRIME.

RESTITUTION (CONTINUED):

THE UNITED STATES GOVERNMENT MANDATED ITS "RESITUTION

PROGRAM BY ENACTING "THE MANDATORY RESTITUTION ACT OF 1996"

(18 U.S.C. SECTION 3663(A). MOST OF THE FIFTY (50) STATES PASSED

SIMILIAR LAWS DURING THE 1990'S. THE MANDATED "RESTITUTION

PROGRAMS" IMPLEMENTED BY THE COURTS AT FEDERAL AND STATE

LEVELS ARE CONFRONTED WITH SIMILIAR ISSUES. THE MOST FREQUENT

PROBLEM ENCOUNTERED IS THE INABILITY OF THE VICTIM TO BE ABLE

TO COLLECT THE "COURT ORDERED RESTITUTION". DEFENDANTS WHO

ARE IN JAIL HAVE NOT FINANCIAL RESOURCES TO PAY THE RESTITUTION.

BOTH THE FEDERAL AND STATE REGULATIONS STIPULATE THAT IF THE

VICTIM RECEIVES PAYMENTS FROM AN APPLICABLE "INSURANCE POLICY"

OR COMPENSATION FROM A STATE'S "VICTIM'S COMPENSATION FUND",

THE RESTITUTION ORDERED TO THE VICTIM WILL BE REASSIGNED TO THE

INSURANCE COMPANY OR THE STATE'S VICTIM'S COMPENSATION

PROGRAM. THE VICTIM IS NOT ALLOWED TO "COLLECT TWICE" FOR THE

SAME CRIMINAL OFFENSE.

VICTIM'S RIGHT TO COMPENSATION

EVERY STATE IN THE UNITED STATES HAS ENACTED SPECIAL

LAWS PROVIDING FOR THE COMPENSATION FOR THE VICTIMS

OF VIOLENT CRIMES. THE TYPE OF CRIMES COVERED BY THESE

ACTS MAY INCLUDE THE FOLLOWING CRIMES:

1. ASSAULT AND BATTERY;
2. SEXUAL ASSAULT/ RAPE;
3. DRUNK DRIVING/DWI;
4. MURDER, 1ST DEGREE;
5. MANSLAUGHTER,
6. NEGLIGENT HOMICIDE;
7. IDENTITY THEFT;
8. CHILD ABUSE/CHILD NEGLECT;
9. HUMAN TRAFFICKING;
10. DOMESTIC VIOLENCE;
11. KIDNAPPING;
12. BURGLARY;
13. CAR JACKING;
14. BREAKING AND ENTERING;
15. LEAVING THE SCENE OF AN ACCIDENT;
16. ACTS OF TERRORISM.
17. ARSON;
18. ROBBERY;
19. CHILD PORNOGRAPHY.

THE LAWS VARY FROM STATE TO STATE. PLEASE CHECK THE GUIDE

(ATTACHED HEREIN) TO FIND THE SPECIFIC LAW IN YOUR STATE.

VICTIM'S COMPENSATION FUNDS

TYPES OF EXPENSES:

1. ALL MEDICAL EXPENSES INCURRED BY THE VICTIM OF THE CRIME IN RECOVERING FROM THE INJURIES SUSTAINED AS A RESULT OF THE CRIME;
2. ALL DENTAL EXPENSES INCURRED BY THE VICTIM;
3. LOST WAGES, (MISSING TIME FROM WORK), DUE TO THE INJURIES SUSTAINED FROM THE CRIME;
4. LOST WAGES WHILE MAKING COURT APPEARANCES TO TESTIFY IN THE CRIMINAL PROCEEDINGS AGAINST THE PERSON ACCUSED OF COMMITTING THE CRIME;
5. FUNERAL EXPENSES (INCURRED BY THE FAMILY OF THE VICTIM) WHERE THE CRIME IS MURDER, MANSLAUGHTER OR NEGLIGENT HOMICIDE;
6. PROPERTY DAMAGES SUSTAINED BY THE VICTIM OF THE CRIME WHERE THERE IS PERSONAL INJURY CRIME;
7. DAMAGES INCURRED AS A RESULT OF A CLEANUP OF THE CRIME SCENE AFTER THE POLICE HAVE COMPLETED THE INVESTIGATION OF THE CRIME SCENE;
8. EXPENSES INCURRED FOR MENTAL HEALTH COUNSELING RESULTING FROM EMOTIONAL, MENTAL ISSUES CAUSED DUE TO BEING THE VICTIM OF A VIOLENT CRIME;

THE LAWS VARY FROM STATE TO STATE. PLEASE CHECK THE GUIDE ATTACHED HERETO TO FIND THE SPECIFIC LAWS IN THE STATE WHERE THE CRIME OCCURRED.

THE FILING OF A CLAIM FOR COMPENSATION

BY THE VICTIM OF A CRIME

THE PROCESS OF FILING OF A CLAIM FOR COMPENATION BY THE VICTIM OF A CRIME REQUIRES THE VICTIM TO TAKE THE FOLLOWING ACTIONS:

1. CONTACT THE STATE AGENCY IN THE STATE WHERE THE CRIME OCCURRED; THE CONTACT INFORMATION SHOULD BE FURNISHED TO THE VICTIM BY THE OFFICE OF THE STATE DISTRICT ATTORNEY OR PROSECUTOR;

2. THE STATE AGENCY IN CHARGE OF A STATE'S VICTIM COMPENSATION PROGRAM MUST FORWARD, (AS REQUIRED) TO THE VICTIM ALL THE APPROPRIATE FORMS INCLUDING THE INSTRUCTION FORMS WITH A THE DETAILED LIST OF ALL THE INFORMATION THAT IS REQUIRED TO COMPLETE THE CLAIM FORMS;

3. UPON RECEIPT OF THE CLAIM FORMS, THE VICTIM MUST DISCLOSE ALL RELEVANT INFORMATION THAT IS REQUIRED IN ORDER FOR THE AGENCY TO PROPERTY INVESTIGATE AND MAKE A DECISION ON THE CLAIM;

4. THE CLAIM FORMS MAY REQUIRE THE VICTIM TO OBTAIN AND FORWARD A COPY OF THE POLICE REPORT OF THE CRIME; MEDICAL RECORDS, LOST WAGE STATEMENTS AND OTHER INFORMATION TO SUPPORT THE CLAIM;

THE STATE AGENCY WILL GENERALLY RULE ON THE MERITS OF THE CLAIM WITHIN 180 DAYS FROM THE FILING OF THE CLAIM.

SAMPLE CLAIM FORM

SECTION A – VICTIM INFORMATION *(Person who was killed, injured, or witnessed)*			
1. Victim's First Name:	**2. Middle Initial:**	**3. Last Name:**	
4. Date of Birth:	**5. Age when the crime was committed:**	**6. Social Security Number:**	**7. Gender:**

8. Street Address, City, State, and Zip Code:

Email:

9. Mailing Address, City, State, and Zip Code *(If different from Street Address):*

10. Daytime Phone: ( )	**11. Other Phone:** ( )

12. Race/Ethnicity: *(For statistical purposes only)*

☐ American Indian or Alaska Native: Tribal Affiliation: _____ ☐ Asian   ☐ Black or African American

☐ Hispanic   ☐ Native Hawaiian or Other Pacific Islander   ☐ White, Non-Latino /Caucasian   ☐ Other Race _____

13. Disabilities Prior to Victimization:

SECTION B – APPLICANT (CLAIMANT) INFORMATION *(Only complete this section if victim is a minor, incapacitated or deceased.)*		
1. Claimant's First Name:	**2. Middle Initial:**	**3. Last Name:**

4. Relationship to the victim shown above:

5. Street Address, City, State, and Zip Code:

Email:

6. Mailing Address, City, State, and Zip Code *(If different from Street Address):*

7. Daytime Telephone: ( )	**8. Other Phone:** ( )	**9. Claimant's SSN:**

SECTION C – INFORMATION ON CONTACT PERSON *(Do not list the victim or claimant or anyone living in the household.)*		
1. Contact's First Name:	**2. Middle Initial:**	**3. Last Name:**

4. Contact's Relationship to Victim:

5. Street Address, City, State, and Zip Code:

6. Mailing Address, City, State, and Zip Code *(If different from Street Address):*

7. Daytime Telephone: ( )	**8. Other Phone:** ( )	**9. Check here if the Contact Person is a Tribal Victim Advocate:** ☐

To Be Completed By VWC

Mailed to Claimant on ___/___/___

VWC Initials _____

Date Rec'd from Clmt. ___/___/___

To Be Completed By OCVCB

Claim #_____

District #_____

V/W Coord. F/R_____

SECTION D - INFORMATION ABOUT THE CRIME

1. What crime was committed which led to the filing of this claim?

- ☐ Arson
- ☐ Assault
- ☐ Burglary
- ☐ Car Jacking
- ☐ DUI/DWI
- ☐ Child Physical Abuse/Neglect (under age 16)
- ☐ Child Pornography (under age 16)
- ☐ Child Sexual Abuse (under age 16)
- ☐ Homicide
- ☐ Human Trafficking
- ☐ Identity Theft/Fraud/Financial Crimes (Only counseling can be compensated for this crime type.)
- ☐ Kidnapping
- ☐ Leaving the Scene
- ☐ Robbery
- ☐ Sexual Assault
- ☐ Stalking
- ☐ Terrorism
- ☐ Other: _____

2. Location of Crime
(Check Primary Location):

- ☐ Bar or Club
- ☐ Business (other than victim's workplace)
- ☐ Rural Area
- ☐ Someone else's apartment/home
- ☐ Street
- ☐ Vehicle
- ☐ Victim's workplace
- ☐ Victim's own apartment/home

☐ Other: _____

City of Crime:
_____

County of Crime:
_____

3. Date of Crime: _____

4. Time of Crime: _____

5. If victim is a child, when was the crime disclosed by the child to an adult: Date: _____ Time: _____

6. When was the crime reported to the police? Date: _____ Time: _____

7. Who reported the crime? _____

8. What agency was the crime reported to? _____

SECTION E - INSURANCE INFORMATION

Is there any insurance coverage to assist with expenses being claimed? ☐ Yes ☐ No   If yes, please list all insurance coverage:

1. Health *(Complete if medical is being claimed)*

Company: _____ Phone: ( ) _____ Member/Group Number: _____

☐ Check here if Medicaid or Soonercare recipient   Medicaid or Soonercare # _____

2. Life Insurance *(Complete if victim is deceased)*

Company: _____ Amount Received: $ _____ Policy Number: _____

Beneficiary: _____ Relationship to victim: _____ Phone: ( ) _____

Address, City, State, Zip: _____

3. Car Insurance *(Complete if the crime was vehicle related)*

Company 1: _____ Amount Received $ _____ Agent Name: _____

Phone ( ) _____ Policy Number: _____ Effective Date: _____

Company 2: _____ Amount Received $ _____ Agent Name: _____

Phone ( ) _____ Policy Number: _____ Effective Date: _____

SECTION F – PRIVATE ATTORNEY INFORMATION: *(COMPLETE IF THERE IS A LAWSUIT. DO NOT INCLUDE CRIMINAL CASE INFORMATION HERE)*

1. Has the victim or claimant filed a *civil* lawsuit against anyone because of this crime ☐ Yes ☐ No

2. Attorney's Name and Law Firm: _____

3. Attorney's Phone: ( ) _____

4. Attorney's Address, City, State, and Zip: _____
_____

How did you hear about this program? (Check One)   ☐ Police   ☐ DA's Office   ☐ Poster/Brochure   ☐ Hospital/Medical Provider
☐ Medical Examiner   ☐ Victim Assistance Program   ☐ Funeral   ☐ Other: _____

SECTION G - VICTIM'S EMPLOYMENT INFORMATION: *(IF SELF-EMPLOYED, TAX RETURNS FOR THE LAST THREE YEARS WILL BE REQUIRED.)*

1. Employer: _____

2. Occupation: _____

3. Employer's Phone: ( ) _____

4. Supervisor's Name: _____

5. Employer's Address, City, State, Zip Code: _____

_____

6. Did the victim miss work due to the crime? ☐ Yes ☐ No

7. How many days of work did the victim miss due to physical or psychological injuries related to the crime? _____

      a. From Date: _____   b. To Date: _____

8. Name of the doctor or mental health professional that released the victim to return to work: _____

9. Doctor or Mental Health Professional's Phone: ( ) _____

10. Doctor or Mental Health Professional's Address, City, State, and Zip Code: _____

_____

SECTION H - DEPENDENTS

Please list the victim's dependents names and ages, if the victim is deceased:

_____

_____

_____

SECTION I - EXPENSES BEING CLAIMED

☐ Funeral / Burial   ☐ Dependent Care / Loss of Support   ☐ Counseling / Mental Health ☐ Travel (doctor/counseling visits)
☐ Traditional American Indian Services   ☐ Medical   ☐ Grief Counseling
☐ Income Loss / Economic Support   ☐ Dental   ☐ Replacement Services
☐ Future Economic Loss   ☐ Rehabilitation   ☐ Crime Scene Cleanup

Information about the Victim's Injuries:
1. List the injuries (physical and psychological) caused by the crime:

_____

_____

2. List doctors, mental health professionals, and hospitals where the victim was, or is receiving treatment after the crime:

_____

_____

3. Funeral Home and address (if applicable): _____

SECTION J - OFFENDER INFORMATION (If known)

1. List those who committed or was charged with the crime(s):

_____

2. Has there been an arrest? ☐ Yes ☐ No   3. Have charges been filed? ☐ Yes ☐ No

4. If charges were filed, what is the Criminal Case Number (if known): _____

5. Relationship of offender to victim (if any): _____

ALABAMA

Eligibility: Victims of Crimes.
Crime must be reported to the police/law enforcement within: 72 Hours.
Criminal charges must be filed within: 1 year.
Exceptions-requirements may be waived for good cause.
Conviction of the crime by the perpetrator is not necessary.

Compensation Provided:

Medical Expenses: Actual Medical Expenses Incurred.
Lost Wages: $400 per week for no more than 26 weeks.
Counseling Services: Up to $8,000 for mental health services.
Moving Expenses: $1,000 in case of imminent danger to the victim.
Travel: Up to $75 per day for trips out of town to coverall court or medical/counseling services.
Funeral Expenses: $5,000
Maximum Amount: $20,000

State Administrative Agency:
Alabama Crime Victims Compensation Commission
5845 Carmichael Drive
P.O. Box 231367
Montgomery, Alabama 36117
1-800-541-9388
344-290-4420
334-290-4455 (Fax)
http://www.acvcc.state.al.us/

ALASKA

Eligibility:
Victims of Crimes.
Crime must be reported 5 days or a reasonable period of time to law enforcement.
Criminal charges must be filed within 2 years.
Exceptions-board weighs reasonableness of requests to waive reporting requirements.
Conviction of the crime by the perpetrator is not necessary.

Compensation Provided:
Medical Expenses
Lost Wages
Counseling Services- $3,380 for child victims. $1,690 for adult primary victims. $1,560 for custodial parents of sexual abuse victims and for child witnesses to domestic violence. $780 for secondary victims.
Moving Expenses-up to $5,000 in relocation costs.
Travel-to obtain medical care, counseling, air ambulance, and to attend court proceedings.
Funeral Expenses-no cap
Maximum Amount-$40,000. In cases of death with multiple dependents up to $80,000.

Administrative Process:
Contact Information-Alaska Violent Crimes Compensation Board
P.O.Box 110230
Juneau, AK 99811-0230
1-800-764-3040
907-465-2379 (Fax)
http://doa.alaska.gov/vccb/

ARKANSAS

Eligibility:
Victims of Crimes.
Crime must be reported to the police/law enforcement within 72 Hours.
Criminal charges must be filed within 1 year.
Exceptions-requirements may be waived for good cause.
Conviction of the crime by the perpetrator is not necessary.

Compensation Provided:
Medical Expenses-up to 65% of charged medical expenses.
Lost Wages-no cap; paid at actual salary.
Counseling Services- $3,500 inpatient and $3,500 for outpatient services.
Travel-no medical transportation cap, plus $300 lodging when directly related to medical and court proceedings.
Funeral Expenses-$7,500
Maximum Amount-$10,000 with an additional $15,000 for catastrophic injury cases.

Administrative Process:
Contact Information-Arkansas Crime Victims Reparations Board
323 Center Street, Suite 600
Little Rock, Arkansas 72201
Toll Free 1-800-448-3014
501-682-1020
501-682-5313 (Fax)
https://arkansasag.gov/public-safety/resources/column-one/crime-victim-reparations/

ARIZONA

Eligibility:
Victims of Crimes.
Crime must be reported to the police/law enforcement within 72 Hours.
Criminal charges must be filed within 2 years.
Exceptions-exceptional circumstances.
Conviction of the crime by the perpetrator is not necessary.

Compensation Provided:
Medical Expenses
Lost Wages-limited up to 40 hours per week at current federal minimum wage law. Work loss up to 40 hours per month for parent of minor victim when accompanying victim for treatment.
Counseling Services- up to 36 months from date of first treatment.
Travel-$1,500 for medical and counseling appointments and to attend court proceedings.
Funeral Expenses-$10,000.
Maximum Amount-$25,000.

Administrative Process:
Contact Info-Arizona Criminal Justice Commission
1110 W. Washington Street, Suite 230
Phoenix, AZ 85007
1-877-668-2252
602-364-1146
602-364-1175 (fax)
http://www.azcjc.gov/

CALIFORNIA

Eligibility:
Victims of Crimes.
There is no set limit for law enforcement reporting period; crime must be reported within a reasonable period of time so that the investigation is not hindered.
Criminal charges must be filed within 3 years; until age 19 for crimes occurring while minors if crimes occurred more than 3 years prior, with limit extended to age 28 if the crime involves sex with a minor.
Exception-good cause exception to the filing period.
Conviction of the crime by the perpetrator is not necessary.

Compensation Provided:
Medical Expenses-medical expenses are generally reimbursed at the Medicare rate; dental expenses are paid at 75%.
Lost Wages-generally limited to 5 years after crime.
Counseling Services- generally limited to 40 sessions for direct victims, 30 sessions for child victims, and 15 sessions for adult indirect victims.
Moving Expenses-up to $2,000 allowed as a one-time cost when recommended by police or therapist.
Funeral Expenses-$5,000.
Maximum Amount-$63,000.

Administrative Process:
Contact Info-California Victim Compensation Board
P.O. Box 3036
Sacramento, CA 95812-3036
1-800-777-9229
916-491-6400 (fax)
https://www.victims.ca.gov/

COLORADO

Eligibility:
Victims of Crimes.
Crime must be reported to the police/law enforcement within 72 Hours.
Criminal charges must be filed within 1 year.
Exceptions-good cause; most boards may waive requirements.
Conviction of the crime by the perpetrator is not necessary.

Compensation Provided: Limits are determined by district.
Medical Expenses
Counseling Services
Lost Wages
Moving Expenses
Funeral Expenses
Travel-if needed for medical treatment.
Emergency: $1,000.
Maximum Amount-$20,000.

Administrative Process: There is a board in each district that meets monthly to consider all claims.
Contact Info-Colorado Office for Victims Programs Division of Criminal Justice
700 Kipling Street, Suite 1000
Denver, CO 80215
303-239-5719
303-239-5743 (fax)
https://www.colorado.gov/pacific/dcj/ovp

CONNECTICUT

Eligibility:
Victims of Crimes.
Crime must be reported to the police/law enforcement within 5 days of crime or when a crime can reasonably by reported.
Criminal charges must be filed within 2 years.
Exceptions-waiver possible for medical, emotional and psychological reasons.
Minimum loss is $100.
Conviction of the crime by the perpetrator is not necessary.

Compensation Provided:
Medical Expenses
Counseling Services
Lost Wages
Emergency-$2,000.
Funeral Expenses-$5,000.
Maximum Amount-$15,000 personal injury claim; $25,000 homicide claim.

Administrative Process:
Contact Info-Connecticut Office of Victim Services
225 Spring Street, 4th Floor
Wethersfield, CT 06109
1-888-286-7347
860-263-2780 (fax)
https://www.jud.ct.gov/crimevictim/

DELAWARE

Eligibility:
Victims of Crimes.
Crime must be reported to the police/law enforcement within 72 hours.
Criminal charges must be filed within 1 year.
Exceptions-extensions to filing may be granted by the board.
Minimum loss is $25.
Conviction of the crime by the perpetrator is not necessary.

Compensation Provided:
Medical Expenses-program has contracts with hospital and other health-care providers to accept 80%
payment as payment in full.
Lost Wages-lost support up to maximum in homicides. Non-Homicide is $3,000.
Counseling Services- for primary victims and family members. Up to $1,200 for children who may be
victims or witnesses.
Moving Expenses-$1,500 for temporary housing for domestic violence victims.
Funeral Expenses-$8,500.
Travel-for medical and counseling if more than 10 miles from victim's residence.
Maximum Amount-$25,000 with additional $25,000 in catastrophic cases.

Administrative Process:
Contact Info-Delaware Victims' Compensation Assistance Program
900 N. King Street, Suite 4
Wilmington, DE 19801
800-464-4357
302-577-1326
http://attorneygeneral.delaware.gov/vcap/

DISTRICT OF COLUMBIA

Eligibility:

Victims of Crimes.

Crime must be reported to the police/law enforcement within 7 days.

Criminal charges must be filed within 1 year or within 1 year of learning of the program with adequate showing that the delay was reasonable.

Exceptions-victims of sexual assault, victims of domestic violence, child cruelty victims.

Conviction of the crime by the perpetrator is not necessary.

Compensation Provided:

Medical Expenses

Counseling Services- $6,000 for children and $3,000 for adults.

Lost Wages-$10,000; $2,5000 per dependent up to total up to $7,500 for support.

Moving Expenses-$1,500 when necessary for health and safety.

Funeral Expenses-$6,000.

Emergency-$1,000.

Maximum Amount-$25,000.

Administrative Process:

Contact Info-District of Columbia Crime Victims Compensation Program

515 5th Street, N.W. #104

Washington, DC 20001

202-879-4216

202-879-4230 (fax)

https://ovsjg.dc.gov/page/crime-victim-compensation

FLORIDA

Eligibility:
Victims of Crimes.
Crime must be reported to the police/law enforcement within 72 hours.
Criminal charges must be filed within 1 year.
Exceptions-for good cause, reporting period may be waived and filing can be extended for 2 years. For crimes against minors, applications can be filed up to 1 year following the victim's 18th birthday or within 2 years for good cause.
Conviction of the crime by the perpetrator is not necessary.

Compensation Provided:
Medical Expenses-provider payment rate of %50 of total bill, up to maximum of $7,500 for up to one year.
Counseling Services- $2,500 for up to 1 year for adults; $7,500 for minor victims or grief counseling; $2,500 for child witnesses to crimes; $7,500 up to one year for in-patient crisis stabilization.
Lost Wages-Up to 66% of salary up to $15,000 for one year; $15,000 in disability cases; lost support up to $25,000.
Moving Expenses-$1,500 for domestic violence victims, with $3,000 lifetime cap.
Funeral Expenses-$5,000.
Travel-for crime related treatment at .29 cents per mile.
Emergency-$1,000.
Maximum Amount-$15,000; with additional $15,000 in catastrophic-injury cases. Note the total treatment costs for medical, dental, and mental health cannot exceed $7,500 per claim.

Administrative Process:
Contact Info-Florida Division of Victim Services and Criminal Justice Programs Office of the Attorney General
The Capital PL-01
Tallahassee, FL 32399
800-226-6667
487-1595 (fax)
http://myfloridalegal.com/victims

GEORGIA

Eligibility:
Victims of Crimes.
Crime must be reported to the police/law enforcement within 72 hours.
Criminal charges must be filed within 1 year.
Exceptions-good cause, requirements liberally applied to child victims.
Conviction of the crime by the perpetrator is not necessary.

Compensation Provided:
Medical Expenses-$15,000.
Counseling Services- $3,000.
Lost Wages-$10,000.
Funeral Expenses-$6,000.
Maximum Amount-$25,000.

Administrative Process:
Contact Info-Georgia Crime Victim Compensation Program Criminal Justice Coordinating Council
104 Marietta Street, Suite 440
Atlanta, GA 30349
800-547-0060
657-1957 (fax)
https://cjcc.georgia.gov/victims-compensation

HAWAII

Eligibility:
Victims of Crimes.
Crime must be reported to the police/law enforcement within 72 hours.
Criminal charges must be filed within 18 months.
Exceptions-may be waived for good cause.
Conviction of the crime by the perpetrator is not necessary.

Compensation Provided:
Medical Expenses-$20,000.
Counseling Services- $10,000; $20,000 for catastrophic cases.
Lost Wages-$3,000.
Moving Expenses-$3,000.
Funeral Expenses-$4,000.
Travel-by air if needed.
Emergency-$1,000.
Maximum Amount-$10,000; up to $20,000 in medical if it exceeds $10,000 limit.

Administrative Process:
Contact Info-Hawaii Crime Victims Compensation Commission
1136 Union Mall, Suite 600
Honolulu, HI 96813
808-587-1143
808-587-1146 (fax)
http://dps.hawaii.gov/cvcc/

IDAHO

Eligibility:
Victims of Crimes.
Crime must be reported to the police/law enforcement within 72 hours.
Criminal charges must be filed within 1 year.
Exceptions-good cause, especially in cases involving minors, domestic violence and sexual assault.
Conviction of the crime by the perpetrator is not necessary.

Compensation Provided:
Medical Expenses
Counseling Services- $2,500 for direct victims, $500 for each family member of homicide and sex assault victims. Additional benefits up to $25,000 for extenuating circumstances.
Lost Wages-$175 per week.
Funeral Expenses-$5,000.
Travel-to obtain treatment.
Emergency Funds
Maximum Amount-$25,000.

Administrative Process:
Contact Info-Idaho Crime Victims Compensation Program
700 South Clearwater Lane
Boise, ID 83712
800-950-2110
208-334-5145 (fax)
https://crimevictimcomp.idaho.gov

ILLINOIS

Eligibility:
Victims of Crimes.
Crime must be reported to the police/law enforcement within 72 hours; 7 days for a sexual assault.
Criminal charges must be filed within 2 years.
Conviction of the crime by the perpetrator is not necessary.

Compensation Provided:
Medical Expenses
Counseling Services
Lost Wages-$1,250 per month.
Moving-temporary lodging and relocation expenses.
Funeral Expenses-$7,500.
Travel-to obtain treatment.
Emergency Funds-$2,000.
Maximum Amount-$27,000.

Administrative Process:
Contact Info-Illinois Court of Claims Crime Victim Compensation Program; Office of the Attorney General
Crime Victims Division
100 West Randolph, 13th Floor
Chicago, IL 60601
800-228-3368
312-814-4231 (fax)
http://www.ag.state.il.us/victims/cvc.html

INDIANA

Eligibility:
Victims of Crimes.
Crime must be reported to the police/law enforcement within 48 hours.
Criminal charges must be filed within 180 days, may be extended to 2 years.
Exceptions-for sex crimes time periods are extended to 2 years.
Minimum loss is $100.
Conviction of the crime by the perpetrator is not necessary.

Compensation Provided:
Medical Expenses
Counseling Services-limit of $1,5000 if therapist charges a sliding scale fee; limit of $1,000 if no sliding scale is used. Limit of $1,000 for family members of victims of homicide, sexual assault, and domestic violence.
Lost Wages
Funeral Expenses-$5,000.
Emergency Funds-$500.
Maximum Amount-$15,000.

Administrative Process:
Contact Info-Violent Crime Victim Compensation Fund, Indiana Criminal Justice Institute
101 W. Washington Street, Suite 1170, East Tower
Indianapolis, IN 46204
800-353-1484
317-233-3912 (fax)
https://www.in.gov/cji/2333.htm

IOWA

Eligibility:
Victims of Crimes.
Crime must be reported to the police/law enforcement within 72 hours.
Criminal charges must be filed within 2 years.
Conviction of the crime by the perpetrator is not necessary.
Exceptions-Intrafamilial child victims have 2 years to file a claim after a report is filed with the Department of Human Services; adults allowed good-cause exception to filing requirement.

Compensation Provided:
Medical Expenses-$25,000 for primary victims; $3,000 for survivors of homicide victims.
Counseling Services-Primary victims $3,000 limit for nonmedical therapy. $3,000 for family members of non-homicide victims.
Lost Wages-$6,000 for disability; $4,000 for dependent in homicide or disability greater than 60 days; $1,000 for court attendance and $1,000 for medical/counseling appointments.
Funeral Expenses-$7,500.
Travel-$1,000 for food and lodging, funeral travel, medical/counseling treatment or court proceedings.
Maximum Amount-No established maximum; each benefit has its own limit.

Administrative Process:
Contact Info-Iowa Crime Victims Assistance Division
Lucas Building, Ground Floor
Des Moines, IA 50319
800-373-5044
515-281-8199 (fax)
https://www.iowaattorneygeneral.gov/for-crime-victims/crime-victim-compensation-program/

LOUISIANA

Eligibility:
Victims of Crimes.
Crime must be reported to the police/law enforcement within 72 hours
Crime must be reported to the police/law enforcement within 72 hours.
Criminal charges must be filed within 1 year.
Conviction of the crime by the perpetrator is not necessary.
Exceptions-good cause; routinely waived for child victims.

Compensation Provided:
Medical Expenses-payment limited to 55% of billed and approved amount.
Counseling Services-26 sessions or 6 months, whichever comes first, with $2,500 for primary victims and secondary victims.
Lost Wages-maximum of $10,000; 52 weeks at maximum of $400 per week gross.
Funeral Expenses-$5,000.
Travel-$300; $500 for air medical evacuation.
Emergency-$500.
Maximum Amount-$10,000; up to $25,000 may be awarded when injuries are total and permanent.

Administrative Process:
Contact Info-Louisiana Crime Victims Reparations Board
P.O. Box 3133
Baton Rouge, LA 70821
1-888-6-VICTIM
225-925-6646 (fax)
http://www.lcle.state.la.us/programs/cvr.asp

KANSAS

Eligibility:
Victims of Crimes.
Crime must be reported to the police/law enforcement within 72 hours. For child sexual assault, period begins on date crime reported to police.
Criminal charges must be filed within 2 years.
Conviction of the crime by the perpetrator is not necessary.
Exceptions-good cause exception for reporting period only.

Compensation Provided:
Medical Expenses
Counseling Services-$3,500; $1,000 for family members in homicide cases; limit of $60 per hour; $10,000 maximum for inpatient care.
Lost Wages-$400 per week.
Funeral Expenses-$5,000.
Travel-to obtain medical assistance.
Moving Expenses-compensable only at recommendation of law enforcement.
Maximum Amount-$25,000.

Administrative Process:
Contact Info-Kansas Crime Victims Compensation Board, Office of the Attorney General
120 S.W. 10th Avenue, 2nd Floor
Topeka, KS 66612-1597
785-296-2359
785-296-0652 (fax)
https://ag.ks.gov/victim-services/victim-compensation

KENTUCKY

Eligibility:
Victims of Crimes.
Crime must be reported to the police/law enforcement within 48 hours.
Criminal charges must be filed 5 years for crimes occurring after July 15, 1998; 1 year for crimes prior to July 15, 1998.
Conviction of the crime by the perpetrator is not necessary.
Exceptions-good cause.

Compensation Provided:
Medical Expenses
Counseling Services
Lost Wages-$150 per week.
Funeral Expenses-$5,000.
Travel-ambulance charges.
Emergency-$500.
Maximum Amount-$25,000.

Administrative Process:
Contact Info-Kentucky Crime Victims Compensation Board
130 Brighton Park Blvd.
Frankfort, KY 40601-3714
1-800-469-2120
502-573-4817 (fax)
http://cvcb.ky.gov/Pages/default.aspx

MAINE

Eligibility:
Victims of Crimes.
Crime must be reported to the police/law enforcement within 5 days.
Criminal charges must be filed within 3 years or within 60 days of discovery of injury or compensable loss whichever is later.
Conviction of the crime by the perpetrator is not necessary.
Exceptions-good cause, with specific exception for child victims.

Compensation Provided:
Medical Expenses-most are paid at 75 % of charges or of balance after insurance payments.
Counseling Services
Lost Wages-including up to $1,000 in lost wages for dependent care.
Funeral Expenses-$5,000; up to $1,000 additional for extraordinary costs in homicides.
Travel-for dependent care.
Maximum Amount-$15,000.

Administrative Process:
Contact Info-Maine Victims' Compensation Program
State House Station #6
Augusta, ME 04333
800-903-7882
207-624-7730 (fax)
http://www.maine.gov/ag/crime/victims_compensation/

MARYLAND

Eligibility:
Victims of Crimes.
Crime must be reported to the police/law enforcement within 72 hours.
Criminal charges must be filed within 3 years.
Conviction of the crime by the perpetrator is not necessary.
Exceptions-good cause, requirements may be waived; requirements will be waived for child victims.

Compensation Provided:
Medical Expenses
Counseling Services-$5,000; up to $1,000 for each family member up to the $5,000 maximum.
Lost Wages-$25,000; with catastrophic, total injury, an additional $25,000 may be awarded; up to 30 days of lost wages for parents caring for an injured child.
Funeral Expenses-$5,000.
Emergency-$2,000.
Maximum Amount-$45,000; additional $25,000 in cases of permanent and total disability.

Administrative Process:
Contact Info-Maryland Criminal Injuries Compensation Board
Suite 206, Plaza Tower Center
6776 Reisterstown Road
Baltimore, MD 21215-2340
888-679-9347
207-624-7730 (fax)
http://www.dpscs.maryland.gov/victimservs/commitment/main_pages/vs-cicb.shtml

MICHIGAN

Eligibility:
Victims of Crimes.
Crime must be reported to the police/law enforcement within 48 hours.
Criminal charges must be filed within 1 year.
Conviction of the crime by the perpetrator is not necessary.
Exceptions-good cause extension for reporting period. Child victims have one year from their majority or, if a minor, from the report of the crime to file application.

Compensation Provided:
Medical Expenses.
Counseling Services-35 hourly sessions; $80 per session maximum for therapist, except $125 per session for psychologist or physician.
Lost Wages-up to $350 weekly.
Funeral Expenses-$5,000; including $500 for grief counseling.
Travel-non local travel costs.
Emergency-$500.
Maximum Amount-$25,000.

Administrative Process:
Contact Info-Michigan Crime Victims Services Compensation
201 Townsend Street
P.O. Box 30195
Lansing, MI 48909
1-877-251-7373
517-373-2439 (fax)
http://www.michigan.gov/mdhhs/0,5885,7-339-71548_54783_54853-14162--,00.html

MINNESOTA

Eligibility:
Victims of Crimes.
Crime must be reported to the police/law enforcement within 30 days.
Criminal charges must be filed within 3 years.
Conviction of the crime by the perpetrator is not necessary.
Exceptions-reporting requirement waived for child abuse and sexual assault victims.

Compensation Provided:
Medical Expenses-paid at 60% of the bill.
Counseling Services-$7,500; paid at 70% of the bill. Secondary victims are eligible for 20 sessions.
Lost Wages-up to 52 weeks of lost wages for victims or parents/spouse of deceased victim. Family members who are primary caregivers for an injured victim may receive up to $2,000 in lost wages. Immediate family members may receive one week of wages to attend funeral. Loss of support paid at $350 per month.
Funeral Expenses-$7,500.
Travel-$1,000 to attend funeral services.
Emergency-$1,500.
Maximum Amount-$50,000.

Administrative Process:
Contact Info-Minnesota Crime Victims Reparations Board
445 Minnesota Street, Suite 2300
St. Paul, MN 55101
888-622-8799
651-296-5787 (fax)
https://dps.mn.gov/divisions/ojp/help-for-crime-victims/Pages/crime-victims-reparations.aspx

MISSISSIPPI

Eligibility:
Victims of Crimes.
Crime must be reported to the police/law enforcement within 72 hours.
Criminal charges must be filed within 36 months.
Exceptions: Reporting requirement may be waived for good cause. In cases of child sexual abuse; application must be filed within 36 months after report is made. Filing requirement may be extended for up to 12 additional months for good cause.
Conviction of the crime by the perpetrator is not necessary.

Compensation Provided:
Medical Expenses-$15,000 ($10,000 for crimes occurring before 7/01/2007).
Counseling Services-$3,500; maximum hourly rate of $120 for M.D., $100 for Ph.D., $80 for licensed professional counselors and licensed clinical social workers.
Lost Wages- $600 per week for a maximum of 52 weeks for the victim and for the claimant to assist the victim during recovery of injuries; one week up to $600 lost wages to attend court proceedings; one week up to $600 to make funeral arrangements.
Funeral Expenses-$6,500 plus transportation costs up to $800 to arrange/attend services if services are at least 45 miles from family members residence.
Relocation-$2,000 for domestic violence victims; $500 for temporary housing for domestic violence victims.
Travel-$800 to obtain medical services or counseling if at least 45 miles from victims residence, $500 to attend funeral services; $1,000 for court proceeding travels; $1,000 to attend execution.
Emergency-$500.
Maximum Amount-$20,000.

Administrative Process:
Contact Info-Mississippi Crime Victim Compensation Program, Office of the Attorney General
P.O. Box 220
Jackson, MS 39205
1-800-829-6766
601-576-4445 (fax)
http://www.ago.state.ms.us/divisions/victim-compensation/

MISSOURI

Eligibility:
Victims of Crimes.
Crime must be reported to the police/law enforcement within 48 hours.
Criminal charges must be filed within 2 years. Exception: child victims have up to 2 years from their 18th birthday within which to file.

Compensation Provided:
Medical Expenses
Counseling Services-$2,500.
Lost Wages-up to $200 per week.
Funeral Expenses-$5,000.
Travel-to obtain medical assistance.
Maximum Amount-$25,000.

Administrative Process:
Contact Info-Missouri Crime Victims' Compensation Program, Department of Public Safety
P. O. Box 1589
Jefferson City, MO 65102-1589
1-800-347-6881
573-526-4940 (fax)
https://dps.mo.gov/dir/programs/cvc/

MASSACHUSETTS

Eligibility:
Victims of Crimes.
Crime must be reported to the police/law enforcement within 5 days.
Criminal charges must be filed within 3 years; to age 21 for minors.
Exceptions-good cause exception for reporting period.
Conviction of the crime by the perpetrator is not necessary.

Compensation Provided:
Medical Expenses
Counseling Services
Lost Wages-
Funeral Expenses-$8,000 for ancillary burial expenses.
Travel-to obtain treatment.
Maximum Amount-$25,000.

Administrative Process:
Contact Info-Massachusetts Victim Compensation and Assistance Division
One Ashburton Place
Boston, MA 02108
617-727-2200 ext. 2160
617-742-6262 (fax)
http://www.mass.gov/ago/public-safety/resources-for-victims/victims-of-violent-crime/victim-compensation.html

MONTANA

Eligibility:
Victims of Crimes.
Crime must be reported to the police/law enforcement within 72 hours.
Criminal charges must be filed within 1 year.
Exceptions-good cause, child victim has 1 year after 18th birthday to file.
Conviction of the crime by the perpetrator is not necessary.

Compensation Provided:
Medical Expenses
Counseling Services- for primary victims, $2,000 or 12 months with possibility of extension (peer review required); secondary victims maximum of $2,000. Per session cost limit is $76.84 per hour for individual therapy.
Lost Wages-2/3 of average gross weekly wage up to ½ of state's average weekly wage (currently $227.03) for employed workers; $100 per week for victim who was unemployed but actively seeking work at the time of injury.
Funeral Expenses-$3,500.
Travel-to obtain medical assistance only if there is no therapist or doctor within 50 miles roundtrip of victim.
Emergency Awards.
Maximum Amount-$25,000.

Administrative Process:
Contact Info-Montana Crime Victims Compensation Program, Office of Victim Services and Restorative Justice
P.O. Box 201410
Helena, MT 59620-1410
1-800-498-6455
406-444-4303 (fax)
https://dojmt.gov/victims/crime-victim-compensation/

NEVADA

Eligibility:
Victims of Crimes.
Crime must be reported to the police/law enforcement within 5 days.
Criminal charges must be filed within 1 year.
Exceptions-good cause exception to extend filing period up to 18 months more; child sexual crime victim has until age 21 to file claim, if crime is reported.
Conviction of the crime by the perpetrator is not necessary.

Compensation Provided:
Medical Expenses-paid according to fee schedule; may be reduced pro-rata.
Counseling Services-$3,000; additional $2,500 available in extreme situations.
Lost Wages-$300 per week.
Funeral Expenses-$5,000.
Travel-to obtain medical assistance; if over 30 miles.
Maximum Amount-$35,000; $150,000 for catastrophic injuries.

Administrative Process:
Contact Info-Nevada Victims of Crime Program
P.O. Box 94525
Las Vegas, NV 89193
702-486-2740
888-941-7890 (fax)
http://voc.nv.gov/Contact/

NEW JERSEY

Eligibility:
Victims of Crimes.
Crime must be reported to the police/law enforcement within 9 months.
Criminal charges must be filed within 3 years.
Exceptions-good cause waiver, child victims may have up to 3 years after age 18.
Conviction of the crime by the perpetrator is not necessary.

Compensation Provided:
Medical Expenses
Counseling Services-$12,500 maximum for direct victim; up to $7,000 for secondary victim.
Lost Wages-$600 per week.
Funeral Expenses-$5,000.
Moving Expenses-$2,500.
Travel-31 cents per mile, up to $10 per day for medical visits and court proceedings; $200 per person up to $1,000 per claim for air/train travel.
Emergency-$5,000.
Maximum Amount-$25,000; supplemental $35,000 for victims with catastrophic injuries.

Administrative Process:
Contact Info-New Jersey Victims of Crime Compensation Office, Department of Law and Public Safety
50 Park Place, 6th Floor
Newark, NJ 07102
800-242-0804
973-648-3937 (fax)
http://www.nj.gov/oag/njvictims/index.html

NEW MEXICO

Eligibility:

Victims of Crimes.

Crime must be reported to the police/law enforcement within 30 days; 180 days for sexual assault and domestic violence victims.

Criminal charges must be filed within 2 years.

Exceptions-child victims must file application within two years of date reported to law enforcement or 18th birthday, whichever comes first.

Compensation Provided:

Medical Expenses-including traditional Native American healing.

Counseling Services-preauthorization required for more than 30 sessions.

Lost Wages

Funeral Expenses-$6,000.

Travel-to obtain treatment.

Maximum Amount-$20,000; up to $50,000 in catastrophic physical injuries.

Administrative Process:

Contact Info-New Mexico Crime Victims Reparation Commission

6200 Uptown, N.E. Suite 210

Albuquerque, NM 87110

800-306-6262

505-841-9437 (fax)

http://www.cvrc.state.nm.us/

NEW HAMPSHIRE

Eligibility:
Victims of Crimes.
Crime must be reported to the police/law enforcement within 1 year.
Criminal charges must be filed within 1 year.
Exceptions-good cause waiver applied in some cases such as sexual assault.
Minimum loss is $100.
Conviction of the crime by the perpetrator is not necessary.

Compensation Provided:
Medical Expenses
Counseling Services-$3,000.
Lost Wages
Funeral Expenses-$5,000.
Relocation Expenses
Travel-to obtain treatment.
Maximum Amount-$25,000.

Administrative Process:
Contact Info-New Hampshire Victims' Assistance Commission Department of Justice
33 Capital Street
Concord, NH 03301
800-300-4500
603-271-2110 (fax)
https://www.doj.nh.gov/grants-management/victims-compensation-program/

NEW YORK

Eligibility:
Victims of Crimes.
Crime must be reported to the police/law enforcement within 7 days.
Criminal charges must be filed within 1 year.
Exceptions-good cause waiver; in claims involving sex offenses or family offenses, police report must be filed within a reasonable time considering all circumstances, including victim's condition and family situation.

Compensation Provided:
Medical Expenses- no maximum.
Counseling Services-no maximum.
Lost Wages-$30,000.
Funeral Expenses-$6,000.
Relocation Expenses-if medically necessary.
Travel-to obtain treatment and for court appearances.
Emergency-$2,500.
Maximum Amount-no maximum for medical expenses; various maximums for other expenses.

Administrative Process:
Contact Info-New York Office of Victim Services
Alfred E. Smith Building
80 South Swan Street, 2nd Floor
Albany, NY 12210
800-247-8035
518-457-8003 (fax)
https://ovs.ny.gov/

NORTH CAROLINA

Eligibility:
Victims of Crimes.
Crime must be reported to the police/law enforcement within 72 hours.
Criminal charges must be filed within 2 years.
Exceptions-good cause exception for reporting period.
Conviction of the crime by the perpetrator is not necessary.

Compensation Provided:
Medical Expenses
Counseling Services-1 year of treatment for adults; 2 years for children 10 and under.
Lost Wages-$300 per week for 26 weeks; in domestic violence cases up to $50 per child lost support
from offender may be paid for up to 26 weeks or until date of employment.
Funeral Expenses-$5,000.
Travel-to obtain treatment.
Maximum Amount-$30,000, plus an additional $3,500 in homicide cases.

Administrative Process:
Contact Info-North Carolina Crime Victims Compensation Commission
4232 Mail Service Center
Raleigh, NC 27699
800-826-6200
919-715-4209
https://www.ncdps.gov/DPS-Services/Victim-Services/Crime-Victim-Compensation

NORTH DAKOTA

Eligibility:
Victims of Crimes.
Crime must be reported to the police/law enforcement within 72 hours.
Criminal charges must be filed within 1 year.
Exceptions-good cause exception; for child abuse and molestation victims, report must be made within 3 years after 18th birthday.
Conviction of the crime by the perpetrator is not necessary.

Compensation Provided:
Medical Expenses-80% of billed charges.
Counseling Services-80% of billed charges.
Lost Wages-$300 per week.
Funeral Expenses-$5,000.
Travel-to obtain treatment.
Emergency awards.
Maximum Amount-$25,000.

Administrative Process:
Contact Info-North Dakota Crime Victims Compensation Program
P.O. Box 5521
Bismark, ND 58506
800-445-2322
701-328-6185 (fax)
https://www.nd.gov/docr/programs/victims/viccomp.html

OHIO

Eligibility:
Victims of Crimes.
There is no limit within which to report the crime.
There is no filing limit.
Exceptions-good cause exception.
Conviction of the crime by the perpetrator is not necessary.

Compensation Provided:
Medical Expenses
Counseling Services-up to overall maximum for primary victim; $2,500 for each immediate family member in homicides; sexual assaults, domestic violence and disabling crimes; with $7,500 aggregate limit.
Lost Wages-includes lost wage of victim to attend trial and in homicides. $500 in lost wages for each immediate family member to attend court proceedings.
Funeral Expenses-$7,500; including up to $500 in travel expenses.
Travel-to obtain treatment and to meet with police and prosecutors.
Moving Expenses.
Maximum Amount-$50,000.

Administrative Process:
Contact Info-Ohio Victims of Crime Compensation Program
150 East Gray Street, 25th Floor
Columbus, OH 43215
877-584-2846
614-752-2732
http://www.ohioattorneygeneral.gov/VictimsCompensation.aspx

OKLAHOMA

Eligibility:
Victims of Crimes.
Crime must be reported to the police/law enforcement within 72 hours.
Criminal charges must be filed within 1 year.
Exceptions-good cause, filing period may be extended no longer than 1 additional year.
Conviction of the crime by the perpetrator is not necessary.

Compensation Provided:
Medical Expenses
Counseling Services-$3,000 limit for primary victims may be waived in extreme cases. For families of homicide victims, limit of $3,000 per person.
Lost Wages-no separate cap for victim's lost wages and support; up to $2,000 in work loss for caregivers.
Funeral Expenses-$6,000.
Travel-to obtain treatment; provided victim had to pay another party for the transportation.
Moving Expenses-in extreme circumstances.
Maximum Amount-$20,000; $40,000 for catastrophic injuries and homicides.

Administrative Process:
Contact Info-Oklahoma Crime Victims Compensation Board District Attorneys Council
421 NW 13th Street, Suite 290
Oklahoma City, OK 73103
800-745-6098
405-264-5097
https://www.ok.gov/dac/Victims/Victims_Compensation_Program/

OREGON

Eligibility:

Victims of Crimes.

Crime must be reported to the police/law enforcement within 72 hours.

Criminal charges must be filed within 6 months.

Exceptions-for child victims, time periods begin at date of disclosure.

Conviction of the crime by the perpetrator is not necessary.

Compensation Provided:

Medical Expenses-$20,000.

Counseling Services-$20,000 for direct victims and family in homicides; $10,000 for children who witness domestic violence; $1,000 for relatives of an Oregon resident who is a victim of international terrorism; $500 for acquaintance or friend of deceased victim who discovered the body.

Lost Wages-$400 per week up to $20,000 limit.

Funeral Expenses-$5,000.

Travel-mileage reimbursement for medical treatment/counseling treatment if over 60 miles round trip. Maximum of $3,000.

Emergency-$1,000.

Maximum Amount-$44,000.

Administrative Process:

Contact Info-Oregon Crime Victims' Services Division, Department of Justice

1162 Court Street, N.E.

Salem, OR 97301

800-503-7983

503-378-5738 (fax)

https://www.doj.state.or.us/crime-victims/

PENNSYLVANIA

Eligibility:
Victims of Crimes.
Crime must be reported to the police/law enforcement within 72 hours.
Criminal charges must be filed within 2 years.
Exceptions-for child victims only.
Conviction of the crime by the perpetrator is not necessary.

Compensation Provided:
Medical Expenses-$35,000; 65% of usual and customary charges.
Counseling Services-$5,000 for adult direct victims; $10,000 for minor direct victims; $5,000 for homicides and $2,500 for non-homicides for non-homicides for relatives of the direct victim.
Lost Wages-maximum of $15,000 in lost wages; $20,000 in lost support.
Funeral Expenses-$6,500 plus transportation expenses.
Moving Expenses-maximum of $1,000 per each direct victim per household per crime.
Travel-to obtain treatment and counseling services; to attend court proceedings; to make funeral arrangements.
Emergency awards-$5,000.
Maximum Amount-$35,000 plus an additional $10,000 for counseling.

Administrative Process:
Contact Info-Pennsylvania Victims Compensation Assistance Program
P.O. Box 1167
Harrisburg, PA 17108
800-233-2339
717-787-4306 (fax)
http://www.pccd.pa.gov/Victim-Services/Pages/Victims-Compensation-Assistance-Program-(VCAP).aspx

RHODE ISLAND

Eligibility:
Victims of Crimes.
Crime must be reported to the police/law enforcement within 10 days.
Criminal charges must be filed within 3 years.
Exceptions-time limits are stayed until child victim reaches age of majority. For adults, good-cause exception to time limits.
Conviction of the crime by the perpetrator is not necessary.

Compensation Provided:
Medical Expenses-paid according to standards of workers' compensation.
Counseling Services
Lost Wages
Funeral Expenses-$8,000.
Travel-to obtain treatment.
Emergency awards-up to $8,000 for burial expenses.
Maximum Amount-$25,000.

Administrative Process:
Contact Info-Rhode Island Crime Victim Compensation, Office of General Treasurer
50 Service Avenue
Warwick, RI 02886
401-462-7655
401-462-7694 (fax)
http://www.treasury.ri.gov/treasury-divisions/crime-victim-compensation-program/

SOUTH CAROLINA

Eligibility:
Victims of Crimes.
Crime must be reported to the police/law enforcement within 48 hours.
Criminal charges must be filed within 180 days.
Exceptions-for good cause, reporting period can be waived; and applicants may file up to 4 years from the crime or the date of its discovery.
Conviction of the crime by the perpetrator is not necessary.

Compensation Provided:
Medical Expenses
Counseling Services-20 sessions or 180 days of treatment.
Lost Wages-based on state worker's compensation rate.
Funeral Expenses-$4,000.
Travel-to obtain medical treatment and counseling.
Emergency awards-$500.
Maximum Amount-$15,000, board may approve additional $10,000 with proper documentation demonstrating financial hardship.

Administrative Process:
Contact Info-South Carolina State Office of Victim Assistance
1205 Pendleton Street, Room 401
Columbia, SC 29201
800-220-5370
803-737-1708 (fax)
http://www.sova.sc.gov/

SOUTH DAKOTA

Eligibility:
Victims of Crimes.
Crime must be reported to the police/law enforcement within 5 days.
Criminal charges must be filed within 1 year.
Exceptions-for good cause waiver applied for children, elderly, domestic violence and sexual assault victims.
Conviction of the crime by the perpetrator is not necessary.

Compensation Provided:
Medical Expenses
Counseling Services-1 year for primary and secondary victims.
Lost Wages-up to 40 hours for parents caring for children.
Funeral Expenses-$6,500.
Travel-mileage reimbursement of up to $720 to obtain medical treatment.
Emergency awards-$1,000.
Maximum Amount-$15,000.

Administrative Process:
Contact Info-South Dakota Crime Victims' Compensation Program
700 Governor's Drive
Pierre, SD 57501-2291
800-696-9476
605-773-6834 (fax)
https://dss.sd.gov/keyresources/victimservices/

TENNESSEE

Eligibility:
Victims of Crimes.
Crime must be reported to the police/law enforcement within 48 hours.
Criminal charges must be filed within 1 year.
Exceptions-reporting and filing periods may be waived.
Conviction of the crime by the perpetrator is not necessary.

Compensation Provided:
Medical Expenses
Counseling Services-up to maximum of $30,000 for direct victims; secondary victims and family members share a cumulative $3,500 per crime.
Lost Wages-85 % of average weekly wage with worker's compensation limits.
Funeral Expenses-$6,000.
Travel-to attend trial, up to 4 claimants may receive up to $1,250.
Emergency awards-$500.
Maximum Amount-$30,000 for crimes occurring on or after July 1, 2000.

Administrative Process:
Contact Info-Tennessee Criminal Injuries Compensation Program Division of Claims Administration
Andrew Jackson Building, 9th Floor
Nashville, TN 37243
615-741-2734
615-532-4979 (fax)
http://treasury.tn.gov/injury/

TEXAS

Eligibility:
Victims of Crimes.
Crime must be reported to the police/law enforcement within a reasonable time period.
Criminal charges must be filed within 3 years.
Exceptions-reporting and filing periods do not apply to child victims; good cause waiver may apply to other cases.
Conviction of the crime by the perpetrator is not necessary.

Compensation Provided:
Medical Expenses-fee schedule places limits on individual procedures.
Counseling Services-$3,000; $400 per day, 30 day limit on inpatient care.
Lost Wages-$500 per week.
Funerals-$4,500.
Moving-for domestic violence victims, one time of up to $2,000 for relocation and $1,800 for rent.
Travel-to obtain treatment and attend court proceedings.
Emergency awards-$1,500.
Maximum Amount-$50,000 with an additional $75,000 for permanent injuries (additional $50,000 for crimes occurring before September 1, 2001).

Administrative Process:
Contact Info-Texas Crime Victims Compensation Program, Victim Services Division, Office of the Attorney General
P.O. Box 12548, Capital Station
Austin, TX 78711
800-983-9933
512-320-8270 (fax)
https://texasattorneygeneral.gov/cvs/crime-victims-compensation-how-to-apply

UTAH

Eligibility:
Victims of Crimes.
Crime must be reported to the police/law enforcement-no time limit.
Filing period-no time limits but crime must have occurred after 1986.
Conviction of the crime by the perpetrator is not necessary.

Compensation Provided:
Medical Expenses-fee schedule places limits on individual procedures.
Counseling Services-$3,500 for primary victims; $2,000 for secondary victims.
Lost wages-$631 per week for up to 12 weeks.
Funerals-$7,000.
Moving-$2,000 for relocation and $1,800 for rent for up to three months for domestic violence and child abuse victims.
Travel-$500 to obtain treatment and attend court proceedings.
Emergency awards
Maximum Amount-$25,000; $50,000 for medical expenses in homicides, attempted homicides, aggravated assault or drunk driving.

Administrative Process:
Contact Info-Utah Office for Victims of Crime
350 East 500 South, Suite 200
Salt Lake City, UT 84111
800-621-7444
801-533-4127 (fax)
https://corrections.utah.gov/index.php?option=com_content&view=article&id=1047&Itemid=166

Vermont

Eligibility:
Victims of Crimes.
There is no set period for law enforcement reporting or for criminal charges to be filed.
Conviction of the crime by the perpetrator is not necessary.

Compensation Provided:
Medical Expenses
Counseling Services-up to 20 sessions with treatment plan, may request extension.
Lost Wages-$2,000 per month maximum for not more than 3 months.
Funeral Expenses-$7,000 plus an additional $2,000 for headstones, cemetery plots, and memorial items.
Travel-gas/mileage to obtain medical treatment and counseling; up to $10,000 in homicides and $2,000 in non-homicides to attend funeral and court proceedings.
Moving Expenses-to include security deposit and rental assistance.
Maximum Amount-$10,000 in homicides, $10,000 for each eligible person.

Administrative Process:
Contact Info-Vermont Center for Crime Victim Services
58 South Main Street, Suite 1
Waterbury, VT 05676-1599
800-750-1213
802-241-1253 (fax)
http://www.ccvs.vermont.gov/

VIRGINIA

Eligibility:

Victims of Crimes.

Crime must be reported to the police/law enforcement within 5 days.

Criminal charges must be filed within 1 year; child sexual assault victims have 10 years past 18th birthday.

Exceptions-for just cause, filing periods may be extended indefinitely for crimes occurring on or after July 1st, 2001.

Conviction of the crime by the perpetrator is not necessary.

Compensation Provided:

Medical Expenses

Counseling Services-no separate maximum for direct victims; $2,500 for each family member in homicides.

Lost Wages-up to 2/3 of average weekly wage not to exceed $600 per week.

Funeral Expenses-$5,000.

Travel-to obtain medical treatment.

Moving Expenses-$1,000.

Emergency awards-based on lost wages.

Maximum Amount-$25,000.

Administrative Process:

Contact Info-Virginia Criminal Injuries Compensation Fund, Worker's Compensation Commission

P. O. Box 26927

Richmond, VA 23261

800-552-4007

804-367-1021 (fax)

http://www.cicf.state.va.us/

WASHINGTON

Eligibility:

Victims of Crimes.

Crime must be reported to the police/law enforcement within 1 year from crime or within 1 year of time report could reasonably have been made.

Criminal charges must be filed within 2 years from report to police; 5 years with good cause.

Exceptions-filing periods for child victims do not start until 18th birthday.

Conviction of the crime by the perpetrator is not necessary.

Compensation Provided:

Medical Expenses-$150,000.

Counseling Services

Lost Wages-$15,000 for lost wages; $40,000 if the victim is permanently and totally disabled. Lost support of up to $40,000 if victim was employed.

Funeral Expenses-$5,750; $6,170 for crimes occurring after July 23, 2017.

Travel-to obtain medical treatment if not available within 15 miles of victim's home.

Maximum Amount-$190,000, with $150,000 in medical benefits and $40,000 in other benefits.

Administrative Process:

Contact Info-Washington Crime Victim Compensation Program, Department of Labor and Industry

P. O. Box 44520

Olympia, WA 98504

800-762-3716

360-902-5333 (fax)

http://www.lni.wa.gov/ClaimsIns/CrimeVictims/

WEST VIRGINIA

Eligibility:
Victims of Crimes.
Crime must be reported to the police/law enforcement within 72 hours.
Criminal charges must be filed within 2 years.
Exceptions-requirements may be waived for good cause; time periods begin with child victims attain age of majority.
Conviction of the crime by the perpetrator is not necessary.

Compensation Provided:
Medical Expenses
Counseling Services-no sublimit for primary and up to $1,000 for secondary victims.
Lost Wages
Funeral Expenses-$10,000.
Travel-to obtain medical treatment; $1,000 for claimants's traveling expenses to prosecute offender.
Moving Expenses-$2,000.
Maximum Amount-$35,000 in personal injury cases; $50,000 in homicides, $100,000 for victims left permanently and totally disabled.

Administrative Process:
Contact Info-West Virginia Crime Victims Compensation Fund West Virginia Court of Claims
1900 Kanawha Blvd, East, Room W-334
Charleston, WV 25305
877-562-6878
304-347-4915 (fax)
http://www.legis.state.wv.us/Joint/victims.cfm

WISCONSIN

Eligibility:
Victims of Crimes.
Crime must be reported to the police/law enforcement within 5 days.
Criminal charges must be filed within 1 year.
Exceptions-for child victims, reporting deadline is 5 days from disclosure, or 18th birthday if adult fails to report on victim's behalf within 5 days of disclosure; filing deadline is 1 year from 18th birthday.
Conviction of the crime by the perpetrator is not necessary.

Compensation Provided:
Medical Expenses
Counseling Services-generally 16 sessions for primary victims and family members in homicides.
Lost Wages-includes lost wages for household/family members to attend funeral.
Funeral Expenses-$2,000.
Emergency-$500.
Maximum Amount-$40,000.

Administrative Process:
Contact Info-Wisconsin Office of Crime Victim Services Department of Justice
P.O. Box 7951
Madison, WI 53707
800-446-6564
608-264-6368 (fax)
https://www.doj.state.wi.us/ocvs

WYOMING

Eligibility:
Victims of Crimes.
Crime must be reported to the police/law enforcement within a reasonable time period.
Criminal charges must be filed within 1 year.
Exceptions-children are given 1 year after the report of the crime to file.
Conviction of the crime by the perpetrator is not necessary.

Compensation Provided:
Medical Expenses
Counseling Services-$4,000 per year for primary victim, $1,500 for associated victim.
Lost Wages-not to exceed federal minimum wage.
Funeral Expenses-$5,000.
Moving-$1,000.
Travel-$600 for travel outside community for medical treatment or counseling, to attend court proceedings, to handle estate matters.
Emergency-$1,000.
Maximum Amount-$15,000, with an additional $10,000 available for catastrophic injuries.

Administrative Process:
Contact Info-Wyoming Division of Victim Services Office of the Attorney General
Herschler Bldg., 1st Floor
122 West 25th Street
Cheyenne, WY 82002
307-777-7200
307-777-6683 (fax)
http://ag.wyo.gov/victim-services-home-page

REGULATIONS ON VICTIMS COMPENSATION

CLAIMS IN EACH OF THE FIFTY (50) STATES:

ALABAMA: WEBSITE: WWW.ACVCC.STATE.AL.US

ALASKA: WEBSITE: WWW.DOA.ALASKA.GOV/VCCB

ARKANSAS: WEBSITE: WWW.ARKANSAS.GOV.PUBLIC-SAFETY.

ARIZONA: WEBSITE: WWW.AZCIC.GOV

CALIFORNIA: WEBSITE: WWW.VICTIM.CA.GOV

COLORADO: WEBSITE: WWW.COLORADO.GOV.PACIFIC.DCJ

CONNECTICUT: WEBSITE: WWW.JUD.CT.GOV/CRIMEVICTIM

DELAWARE: WEBSITE: WWW.ATTORNEY.GENERAL.DELAWARE.GOV

FLORIDA: WEBSITE: WWW.MYFLORIDA.LEGAL.COM.VICTIMS

GEORGIA: WEBSITE: WWW.CJCC.GEORGIA.GOV.VICTIMS

HAWAII: WEBSITE: WWW.DPS.HAWAII.GOV.CVCC

IDAHO: WEBSITE: WWW.CRIME.VICTIM.COMP.IDAHO.GOV

ILLINOIS: WEBSITE: WWW.AG.STATE.IL.US.CVC

INDIANA: WEBSITE: WWW.IN.GOV.CJI.2333

IOWA: WEBSITE: WWW.IOWA.ATTORNEYGENERAL.GOV.CVC.

LOUISANA: WEBSITE: WWW.LCLE.STATE.LA.US.PROGRAMS.CVR

KANSAS: WEBSITE: WWW.AG.KS.GOV.VICTIMS.SERVICES

KENTUCKY WEBSITE: WWW.CVCB.KY.GOV

STATE REGULATIONS (CONTINUED):

MAINE: WEBSITE: WWW.MAINE.GOV.AG.CRIME.VICTIMS

MARYLAND: WEBSITE: WWW.DPSCS.MARYLAND.VICTIMS.GOV

MICHIGAN: WEBSITE: WWW.MICHIGAN.GOV.MDHHS

MINNESOTA: WEBSITE: WWW.OPS.MN.GOV.OJP

MISSISSIPPI: WEBSITE: WWW.AGO.STATE.MS.US.VICTIMS

MISSOURI: WEBSITE: WWW.DPS.MO.GOV.CVCC

MASSACHUSETTS: WEBSITE: WWW.MASS.GOV.AGO.VICTIMS

MONTANA: WEBSITE: WWW.DOJMT.GOV.VICTIMS

NEVADA: WEBSITE: WWW.VOC.NV.GOV

NEW JERSEY: WEBSITE: WWW.NJ.GOV.OAG.VICTIMS

NEW MEXICO: WEBSITE: WWW.CVRC.STATE.NM.US

NEW HAMPSHIRE: WEBSITE: WWW.DOJ.NH.GOV.VICTIMS

NEW YORK: WEBSITE: WWW.OVS.NY.GOV

NORTH CAROLINA: WEBSITE: WWW.NCDPS.GOV

NORTH DAKOTA: WEBSITE: WWW.ND.GOV.VICTIMS

OHIO: WEBSITE: WWW.OHIO.ATTORNEYGENERAL.GOV.VICTIMS

OKLAHOMA: WEBSITE: WWW.OK.GOV.DAC.VICTIMS

OREGON: WEBSITE: WWW.DOJ.STATE.OR.US.VICTIMS

PENNSYLVANIA: WEBSITE: WWW.PCCD.PA.GOV.VICTIMS

STATE REGULATIONS (CONTINUED):

RHODE ISLAND: WEBSITE: WWW.TREASURY.RI.GOV.VICTIMS

SOUTH CAROLINA: WEBSITE: WWW.SOVA.SC.GOV

SOUTH DAKOTA: WEBSITE: WWW.DSS.SD.GOV.VICTIMS

TENNESSEE: WEBSITE: WWW.TREASURY.TN.GOV.INJURY

TEXAS WEBSITE: WWW.TEXAS.AG.CVS.VICTIMS

UTAH: WEBSITE: WWW.CORRECTIONS.UTAH

VERMONT: WEBSITE: WWW.CCVS.VERMONT.GOV

VIRGINIA: WEBSITE: WWW.CICF.STATE.VA.US

WASHINGTON: WEBSITE: WWW.INI.WA.GOV.VICTIMS

WEST VIRGINIA: WEBSITE: WWW.LEGIS.STTE.WV.US.VICTIMS

WISCONSIN: WEBSITE: WWW.DOJ.STATE.WI.US.OCVS

WYOMING: WEBSITE: WWW.AG.WYO,GOV.VICTIMS

BIBLIOGRAPHY

A. MIRANDA V. ARIZONA, 384 U.S. 436 (1966).

B. MAPP V. OHIO, 367 U.S. 644 (1961).

C. GIDEON V. WAINWRIGHT, 372 U.S. 335 (1963).

D. COLORADO V. CONNELLY, 479 U.S. 457 (1986).

E. CALIFORNIA V. GREENWOOD, 486 U.S. 35 (1988).

F. ILLINOIS V. GATES, 462 U.S. 213 (1983).

G. SOUTH DAKOTA V. OPPERMAN, 428 U.S. 364 (1976).

H. TERRY V. OHIO, 392 U.S. 1 (1968).

I. SCHMERBER V. CALIFORNIA, 384 U.S. 757 (1966).

J. TENNESSEE V. GARNER, 471 U.S. 1 (1985).

K. KYLLO V. U.S. GOVERNMENT, 533 U.S. 27 (2001).

L. KATZ V. U.S. GOVERNMENT, 389 U.S. 347 (1967).

M. CHIMEL V. CALIFORNIA, 395 U.S. 752 (1969).

N. U.S. GOVERNMENT V. JACOBSEN, 466 U.S. 109 (1984).

O. PAYNE V. TENNESSEE, 501 U.S. 808 (1991).

P. VIOLENT CRIME CONTROL ACT (1984), 18 U.S.C. SECTION 1033.

Q. 6TH AMENDMENT, U.S. CONSTITUTION, (1789).

R. THE VICTIM'S RIGHT ACT (2004), 18 U.S. CODE, SECTION 3771.

S. VICTIMS OF CRIME ACT (1984), 42 U.S.C. 112.

T. "THE HISTORY OF VICTIM'S RIGHTS IN AMERICA",
   THE NATIONAL CRIME INSTITUTE, (2014).

U. "THE JUSTICE FOR ALL ACT" (2004), 18 U.S.C. SECTION 3771.

V. "THE MANDATORY RESTITUTION ACT" 18 U.S.C. SECTION 3663(A).

JUVENILE

CRIME

THE COURT PROCESS

THE VICTIM OF A JUVENILE ACT OF VANDALISM HAS A CIVIL REMEDY AGAINST THE JUVENILE'S PARENTS. A PERSON INJURED IN AN AUTO ACCIDENT WITH A JUVENILE HAS A SIMILAR REMEDY AGAINST THE PARENTS OF THE JUVENILE. THE AMOUNT OF THE RECOVERY (ESTABLISHED BY THE LAW OF THE STATE IN WHICH THE VICTIM LIVES) DETERMINES THE CIVIL PROCESS THAT THE VICTIM MUST PURSUE IN ORDER TO RECOVER THE SPECIFIED DAMAGES. EACH STATE'S LAW MAY PLACE LIMITS ON THE AMOUNT OF THE RECOVERY WHICH HAS A SIGNIFICANT IMPACT ON THE VICTIM'S CLAIM. IF THE STATE LAW LIMITS THE RECOVERY TO A SMALL AMOUNT, ($1,500.00 TO $2,500.00) THE VICTIM MAY INSTITUTE THE ACTION IN THE STATE'S SMALL CLAIMS COURT. SMALL CLAIMS COURT ALLOWS THE VICTIM TO APPEAR BEFORE THE ASSIGNED JUDGE AND PRESENT THEIR EVIDENCE OF THE VANDALISM OR AUTOMOBILE ACCIDENT IN A SHORT PERIOD OF TIME, TYPICALLY 30 TO 60 DAYS AFTER THE FILING OF THE CASE. THE JUDGE WILL HEAR THE PARTIES' EVIDENCE AND RENDER A DECISION IMMEDIATELY. A JUDGMENT IN FAVOR OF THE VICTIM CAN BE FILED OF RECORD AND SERVE AS LIEN AGAINST ANY PROPERTY OWNED BY THE PARENTS. THE JUDGMENT, IF UNPAID BY THE RESPONSIBLE PARENT, CAN BE USED AS THE BASIS OF A GARNISHMENT AGAINST THE PARENTS WAGES OR AN EXECUTION AGAINST ANY REAL OR PERSONAL PROPERTY BELONGING TO THE PARENT THAT IS NOT EXEMPT BY THE APPLICABLE LAW OF THAT STATE.

CIVIL COURT PROCESS

A STATE'S LAW MAY PROVIDE THAT THE VICTIM CAN RECOVER MORE THAN $2,500.00. IF THE LAW PROVIDES FOR A LARGER RECOVERY OF DAMAGES, THE VICTIM WILL BE REQUIRED TO INSTITUTE A CIVIL ACTION IN THE APPLICABLE COURT WITH JURISDICTION AND SERVE THE PARENT WITH A CIVIL SUMMONS TO ANSWER TO THE VICTIM'S CLAIM AND APPEAR IN COURT. THE COURT PROCESS IN A DISTRICT COURT CIVIL CASE TYPICALLY TAKES TWELVE TO TWENTY-FOUR MONTHS BEFORE THE CASE CAN BE HEARD BY THE COURT. THE VICTIM WILL BE REQUIRED TO HIRE AN ATTORNEY TO REPRESENT THEM IN THE COURT PROCEEDING. SINCE ATTORNEYS MAY CHARGE FOR THEIR SERVICES, THE EXPENSE, OF HIRING AN ATTORNEY, MAY EXCEED THE AMOUNT OF DAMAGES THAT THE VICTIM CAN RECOVER IN THE CASE. SOME STATE LAWS PROVIDE THAT IF THE VICTIM MAKES A RECOVERY, THE ATTORNEY'S FEES INCURRED BY THE VICTIM MAY BE AWARDED AS DAMAGES IN ADDITION TO THE VICTIM'S ACTUAL LOSS. (CHECK THE GUIDE AT THE END OF THIS CHAPTER) TO DETERMINE WHERE THE VICTIM'S ATTORNEYS FEES MAY BE RECOVERED AS A PART OF THE EXPENSE OF FILING THE CASE. ONCE THE JUDGMENT IS FINAL, THE ATTORNEY WILL BE ALLOWED TO EXECUTE ON THE PARENT'S NONEXEMPT PROPERTY TO COLLECT ON THE COURT JUDGMENT. ANY JUDGMENT IS VALID AGAINST THE PARENT FOR A MINIMUM OF FIVE YEARS AND CAN BE RENEWED FOR AN EXTENTION OF TEN YEARS OR LONGER.

JUVENILES AND VANDALISM

ONE OF THE SIGNIFICANT ISSUES IN AMERICAN SOCIETY IS THE PROBLEM OF JUVENILES WHO DAMAGE OTHER CITIZEN'S PROPERTY THROUGH ACTS OF VANDALISM OR THE CARELESS OPERATION OF A MOTOR VEHICLE. JUVENILES CAN NOT BE HELD "LIABLE" IN A COURT OF LAW FOR ANY DAMAGES THAT THEY MAY CAUSE TO OTHER CITIZEN'S PROPERTY. A JUVENILE (PERSONS UNDER 18 YEARS OF AGE), DOES NOT HAVE THE "LEGAL CAPACITY" TO BE SUED IN A COURT OF LAW IN AMERICAN SOCIETY. IN LIGHT OF THIS LEGAL BARRIER, MOST STATES HAVE ENACTED LAWS IMPOSING DIRECT LIABILITY UPON THE PARENTS OF A JUVENILE WHO CAUSES DAMAGE TO A CITIZEN'S PROPERTY. TO DETERMINE THE REGULATIONS FOR A PARTICULAR STATE, PLEASE CONSULT THE GUIDE CONTAINED HEREIN. EACH OF THE FIFTY STATES HAVE DISTINCT LAWS WITH REGARD TO THE FINANCIAL LIABILITY OF THE PARENTS AND THE TYPES OF DAMAGES THAT MAY BE RECOVERED FROM THE PARENTS OF A JUVENILE OFFENDER.

THE STANDARD OF PROOF

THE VICTIM OF A JUVENILE'S VANDALISM OR CARELESS OPERATION OF A MOTOR VEHICLE HAS A SPECIFIC REMEDY AGAINST THE PARENTS OF THE JUVENILE. THE CIVIL ACTION MUST BE FILED AGAINST THE PARENTS OF THE JUVENILE IN THE DISTRICT COURT WHERE THE VICTIM LIVES OR WHERE THE PROPERTY OF THE VICTIM IS LOCATED. IN THIS CIVIL ACTION, THE VICTIM MUST IDENTIFY THE PARENTS OF THE JUVENILE AND PROVE THE ACTUAL DAMAGES CAUSED BY THE JUVENILE. THE BURDEN OF PROOF IN THE CIVIL ACTION IS "BY A PREPONDERANCE OF THE EVIDENCE". THIS LEGAL RULE REQUIRES THE VICTIM TO SHOW THAT "MORE LIKELY THAN NOT", THE JUVENILE CAUSED THE DAMAGE TO THE VICTIM'S PERSON OR PROPERTY. THE LEGAL LIABILITY OF THE PARENTS IS PREDICATED ON THE LEGAL THEORY THAT THE PARENT FAILED TO ADEQUATELY SUPERVISE THE JUVENILE LIVING AT THE HOME OF THE PARENT.

AUTOMOBILE ACCIDENTS

SOME STATES HAVE ESTABLISHED CODIFIED STATE LAWS TO ALLOW CITIZENS, (INJURED IN AN AUTOMOBILE ACCIDENT WITH A JUVENILE), TO FILE A CIVIL ACTION DIRECTLY AGAINST THE PARENTS OF THE JUVENILE DRIVER. THE LEGAL THEORY, IMPOSED BY THE COURT SYSTEM IN THESE STATES, IS THAT THE PARENTS HAVE A LEGAL REPONSIBILTIY TO PROPERLY SUPERVISE THEIR CHILDREN IN THEIR OPERATION OF THE FAMILY AUTOMOBILE. THE FUNDAMENTAL DOCTRINE IN THOSE STATES IS THAT THE LIABILITY OF THE PARENT IS PREDICATED ON THE PARENT WHO HAS SIGNED THE JUVENILE'S APPLICATION TO OBTAIN HIS DRIVER'S LICENSE. THE PARENT IS THUS LEGALLY REQUIRED TO EXERCISE PROPER OVERSIGHT OF THE JUVENILE IN THE OPERATION OF THE FAMILY AUTOMOBILE. THE LEGAL LIMITS OF THE PARENT'S LIABILITY IS GENERALLY BASED ON THE LIABILTY LIMITS OF THE AUTOMOBILE INSURANCE POLICY THAT THE PARENT IS REQUIRED BY LAW TO MAINTAIN ON THE FAMILY AUTOMOBILE. (CONSULT THE GUIDE AT THE END OF THIS CHAPTER TO DETERMINE THE LEGAL LIABILTY OF THE PARENT).

THE DAMAGES

THE VICTIM IS ALLOWED TO RECOVER ALL ACTUAL DAMAGES THAT THEY SUSTAIN AS A RESULT OF THE JUVENILE'S ACT OF VANDALISM OR CARELESS DRIVING OF THE FAMILY AUTO. THESE DAMAGES MAY INCLUDE THE COSTS OF REPAIRS TO THE PROPERTY; THE LOSS OF USE OF THE PROPERTY DURING THE TIME THAT THE PROPERTY COULD NOT BE USED. IN THE EVENT THAT THE PROPERTY IS TOTALLY DESTROYED, THE PROPERTY OWNER MAY RECOVER THE MAXIMUM AMOUNT ALLOWED UNDER THAT STATE'S LAW. IN THE EVENT THAT THE VICTIM IS INJURED AS A RESULT OF THE JUVENILE'S VANDALISM OR CARELESS DRIVING, THE VICTIM MAY RECOVER MEDICAL EXPENSES, DAMAGES FOR PAIN AND SUFFERING AND LOST WAGES FROM MISSING TIME FROM WORK. IN ADDITION TO THE VICTIM'S DAMAGES, THE COURT WILL ALLOW THE VICTIM TO RECOVER ANY AND ALL COURT COSTS INCURRED BY THE VICTIM IN FILING THE LEGAL ACTION AGAINST THE PARENTS. (SEE THE GUIDE AT THE END OF THIS CHAPTER TO DETERMINE THE AMOUNT ALLOWED IN EACH STATE).

THE COURT PROCESS

THE AMOUNT OF THE RECOVERY OF THE VICTIM'S DAMAGES PERMITTED IN A PARTICULAR STATE DETERMINES THE COURT PROCESS THAT IS REQUIRED TO MAKE A RECOVERY. A FEW STATES PLACE A LEGAL LIMIT OF NO MORE THAT $2500.00 DOLLARS CAN BE RECOVERED AGAINST THE PARENTS OF THE JUVENILE. IN THOSE STATES, THE VICTIM WILL BE ALLOWED TO FILE A "SMALL CLAIMS ACTION" DIRECTLY AGAINST THE RESPONSIBLE PARENT. SMALL CLAIMS COURT HEARINGS ARE CONDUCTED IN A RELATIVELY SHORT PERIOD OF TIME (WITHIN 30 TO 60 DAYS). THE SMALL CLAIMS JUDGE WILL CONDUCT A SUMMARY HEARING AND MAKE A RULING THAT DAY. MOST STATES HAVE ENACTED STATE LAWS IMPOSING LIABILITY ON THE PARENTS FOR AMOUNTS UP TO $25,000.00. THESE TYPES OF CIVIL ACTION TYPICALLY REQUIRE THE VICTIM TO HIRE AN ATTORNEY TO REPRESENT THEM IN THE COURT PROCEEDING. MOST STATE LAWS PROVIDE THAT THE COURT MAY ASSESS ATTORNEY FEES INCURRED BY THE VICTIM AGAINST THE PARENTS OF THE JUVENILE AS PART OF THE CASE.

COLLECTING THE JUDGMENT

ONCE A JUDGMENT IS ENTERED FOR THE VICTIM AGAINST THE RESPONSIBLE PARENT, THE JUDGMENT IS ENTERED "OF RECORD" AGAINST THE PARENT. SUCH A JUDGMENT CONSTITUTES A LIEN AGAINT THE DEFENDANT PARENT'S PROPERTY AND ASSETS. AFTER A PERIOD OF 30 DAYS, THE JUDGMENT BECOMES A "FINAL JUDGMENT". THE VICTIM HAS A RIGHT TO TAKE LEGAL STEPS TO COLLECT ON THE JUDGMENT. THE VICTIM MAY HAVE THE SHERIFF'S DEPARTMENT CONDUCT AN "EXECUTION" ON THE PARENT'S PROPERTY. ANY NONEXEMPT ASSETS CAN BE TAKEN BY THE SHERIFF'S OFFICE AND SOLD AT A PUBLIC AUCTION TO SATISFY THE VICTIM'S JUDGMENT. THE VICTIM MAY ALSO HAVE THE CLERK OF THE COURT ISSUE A GARNISHMENT AGAINST THE PARENT'S BANK ACCOUNTS OR PLACE OF EMPLOYMENT IN ORDER TO COLLECT ON THE JUDGMENT. IN THE EVENT THAT THE COURT PROCESS IN AN EXECUTION OR GARNISHMENT DOES NOT SATISFY THE JUDGMENT, THE VICTIM MAY REQUEST A "HEARING ON ASSETS" BEFORE THE ASSIGNED JUDGE. THE HEARING WOULD LIKE RESULT IN THE PARENT BEING ORDERED TO MAKE A MONTHLY PAYMENT TO SATISFY THE JUDGMENT.

ALABAMA

1. ELIGIBILITY: VICTIMS OF JUVENILE CRIMES.

2. CRIME: MUST BE REPORTED TO LOCAL POLICE.

3. CRIMINAL CHARGES: MUST BE FILED WITHIN ONE (1) YEAR.

4. CONVICTION: THE JUVENILE NEED NOT BE CONVICTED OF THE THE CRIME IN ORDER FOR THE VICTIM TO RECOVER DAMAGES.

5. STATUTE: ALABAMA CODE: A.C., # 6—5—380 (1975)

6. TYPES OF DAMAGES ALLOWED: DAMAGES TO REAL PROPERTY OF THE VICTIM OR THE VICTIM'S PERSONAL INJURIES.

7. LIMITS ON RECOVERY: $1,000.00 FOR AN ACT OF VANDALISM AND $1,000.00 FOR A VICTIM'S PERSONAL INJURIES.

8. APPLICATION: APPLIES TO ALL JUVENILES UNDER AGE 18.

9. PARTIES RESPONSIBLE: PARENTS OF JUVENILE; LEGAL GUARDIANS APPOINTED BY THE COURT TO OVERSEE THE WELFARE OF THE JUVENILE.

10. ACTION FOR RECOVERY: THE VICTIM FILES A "CIVIL ACTION" IN THE STATE COURT WHERE THE VICTIM LIVES OR WHERE THE PROPERTY IS LOCATED.

ALASKA

1. ELIGIBILITY: VICTIMS OF JUVENILE CRIMES.

2. CRIME: MUST BE REPORTED TO LOCAL POLICE.

3. CRIMINAL CHARGES: MUST BE FILED WITHIN ONE (1) YEAR.

4. CONVICTION: THE JUVENILE NEED NOT BE CONVICTED OF THE THE CRIME IN ORDER FOR THE VICTIM TO RECOVER DAMAGES.

5. STATUTE: ALASKA CODE: #09.65.255 & 28.15.071.

6. TYPES OF DAMAGES ALLOWED: DAMAGES TO REAL PROPERTY OF THE VICTIM OR THE VICTIM'S PERSONAL INJURIES.

7. LIMITS ON RECOVERY: $15,000.00 FOR AN ACT OF VANDALISM AND $25,000.00 FOR A VICTIM'S PERSONAL INJURIES.

8. APPLICATION: APPLIES TO ALL JUVENILES UNDER AGE 18.

9. PARTIES RESPONSIBLE: PARENTS OF JUVENILE; LEGAL GUARDIANS APPOINTED BY THE COURT TO OVERSEE THE WELFARE OF THE JUVENILE.

10. ACTION FOR RECOVERY: THE VICTIM FILES A "CIVIL ACTION" IN THE STATE COURT WHERE THE VICTIM LIVES OR WHERE THE PROPERTY IS LOCATED.

ARIZONA

1. **ELIGIBILITY: VICTIMS OF JUVENILE CRIMES.**

2. **CRIME: MUST BE REPORTED TO LOCAL POLICE.**

3. **CRIMINAL CHARGES: MUST BE FILED WITHIN ONE (1) YEAR.**

4. **CONVICTION: THE JUVENILE NEED NOT BE CONVICTED OF THE THE CRIME IN ORDER FOR THE VICTIM TO RECOVER DAMAGES.**

5. **STATUTE: ARIZONA CODE: # 12.661.**

6. **TYPES OF DAMAGES ALLOWED: DAMAGES TO REAL OR PROPERTY OWNED BY THE VICTIM.**

7. **LIMITS ON RECOVERY: $10,000.00 FOR ACTS OF VANDALISM; AND $10,000.00 FOR AUTO ACCIDENTS INVOLVING THE JUVENILE.**

8. **APPLICATION: APPLIES TO ALL JUVENILES UNDER AGE 18.**

9. **PARTIES RESPONSIBLE: PARENTS OF JUVENILE; LEGAL GUARDIANS APPOINTED BY THE COURT TO OVERSEE THE WELFARE OF THE JUVENILE.**

10. **ACTION FOR RECOVERY: THE VICTIM FILES A "CIVIL ACTION" IN THE STATE COURT WHERE THE VICTIM LIVES OR WHERE THE PROPERTY IS LOCATED.**

ARKANSAS

1. ELIGIBILITY: VICTIMS OF JUVENILE CRIMES.

2. CRIME: MUST BE REPORTED TO LOCAL POLICE.

3. CRIMINAL CHARGES: MUST BE FILED WITHIN ONE (1) YEAR.

4. CONVICTION: THE JUVENILE NEED NOT BE CONVICTED OF THE THE CRIME IN ORDER FOR THE VICTIM TO RECOVER DAMAGES.

5. STATUTE: ARKANSAS CODE: # 09-25-102.

6. TYPES OF DAMAGES ALLOWED: DAMAGES TO REAL OR PROPERTY OWNED BY THE VICTIM.

7. LIMITS ON RECOVERY: $5,000.00 FOR ACTS OF VANDALISM; AND $5,000.00 FOR AUTO ACCIDENTS INVOLVING THE JUVENILE.

8. APPLICATION: APPLIES TO ALL JUVENILES UNDER AGE 18.

9. PARTIES RESPONSIBLE: PARENTS OF JUVENILE; LEGAL GUARDIANS APPOINTED BY THE COURT TO OVERSEE THE WELFARE OF THE JUVENILE.

10. ACTION FOR RECOVERY: THE VICTIM FILES A "CIVIL ACTION" IN THE STATE COURT WHERE THE VICTIM LIVES OR WHERE THE PROPERTY IS LOCATED.

CALIFORNIA

1. ELIGIBILITY: VICTIMS OF JUVENILE CRIMES.

2. CRIME: MUST BE REPORTED TO LOCAL POLICE.

3. CRIMINAL CHARGES: MUST BE FILED WITHIN ONE (1) YEAR.

4. CONVICTION: THE JUVENILE NEED NOT BE CONVICTED OF THE THE CRIME IN ORDER FOR THE VICTIM TO RECOVER DAMAGES.

5. STATUTE: CALIFORNIA CODE: #1714.1-3 & #17707-17708.

6. TYPES OF DAMAGES ALLOWED: DAMAGES TO REAL PROPERTY OF THE VICTIM OR THE VICTIM'S PERSONAL INJURIES.

7. LIMITS ON RECOVERY: $25,000.00 FOR AN ACT OF VANDALISM ON REAL PROPERTY AND UP TO 30,000.00 FOR PERSONAL INJURIES.

8. APPLICATION: APPLIES TO ALL JUVENILES UNDER AGE 18.

9. PARTIES RESPONSIBLE: PARENTS OF JUVENILE; LEGAL GUARDIANS APPOINTED BY THE COURT TO OVERSEE THE WELFARE OF THE JUVENILE.

10. ACTION FOR RECOVERY: THE VICTIM FILES A "CIVIL ACTION" IN THE STATE COURT WHERE THE VICTIM LIVES OR WHERE THE PROPERTY IS LOCATED.

COLORADO

1. ELIGIBILITY: VICTIMS OF JUVENILE CRIMES.

2. CRIME: MUST BE REPORTED TO LOCAL POLICE.

3. CRIMINAL CHARGES: MUST BE FILED WITHIN ONE (1) YEAR.

4. CONVICTION: THE JUVENILE NEED NOT BE CONVICTED OF THE THE CRIME IN ORDER FOR THE VICTIM TO RECOVER DAMAGES.

5. STATUTE: COLORADO CODE: #13-21-107-107.5 & #42-2-108.

6. TYPES OF DAMAGES ALLOWED: DAMAGES TO REAL PROPERTY OF THE VICTIM OR THE VICTIM'S PERSONAL INJURIES.

7. LIMITS ON RECOVERY: $3,500.00 FOR AN ACT OF VANDALISM AND $3,500.00 FOR A VICTIM'S PERSONAL INJURIES.

8. APPLICATION: APPLIES TO ALL JUVENILES UNDER AGE 18.

9. PARTIES RESPONSIBLE: PARENTS OF JUVENILE; LEGAL GUARDIANS APPOINTED BY THE COURT TO OVERSEE THE WELFARE OF THE JUVENILE.

10. ACTION FOR RECOVERY: THE VICTIM FILES A "CIVIL ACTION" IN THE STATE COURT WHERE THE VICTIM LIVES OR WHERE THE PROPERTY IS LOCATED.

CONNECTICUT

1. **ELIGIBILITY: VICTIMS OF JUVENILE CRIMES.**

2. **CRIME: MUST BE REPORTED TO LOCAL POLICE.**

3. **CRIMINAL CHARGES: MUST BE FILED WITHIN ONE (1) YEAR.**

4. **CONVICTION: THE JUVENILE NEED NOT BE CONVICTED OF THE THE CRIME IN ORDER FOR THE VICTIM TO RECOVER DAMAGES.**

5. **STATUTE: CONNECTICUT CODE: #52-572.**

6. **TYPES OF DAMAGES ALLOWED: DAMAGES TO REAL PROPERTY OF THE VICTIM OR THE VICTIM'S PERSONAL INJURIES.**

7. **LIMITS ON RECOVERY: $5,000.00 FOR AN ACT OF VANDALISM AND $5,000.00 FOR A VICTIM'S PERSONAL INJURIES.**

8. **APPLICATION: APPLIES TO ALL JUVENILES UNDER AGE 18.**

9. **PARTIES RESPONSIBLE: PARENTS OF JUVENILE; LEGAL GUARDIANS APPOINTED BY THE COURT TO OVERSEE THE WELFARE OF THE JUVENILE.**

10. **ACTION FOR RECOVERY: THE VICTIM FILES A "CIVIL ACTION" IN THE STATE COURT WHERE THE VICTIM LIVES OR WHERE THE PROPERTY IS LOCATED.**

DELAWARE

1. ELIGIBILITY: VICTIMS OF JUVENILE CRIMES.

2. CRIME: MUST BE REPORTED TO LOCAL POLICE.

3. CRIMINAL CHARGES: MUST BE FILED WITHIN ONE (1) YEAR.

4. CONVICTION: THE JUVENILE NEED NOT BE CONVICTED OF THE THE CRIME IN ORDER FOR THE VICTIM TO RECOVER DAMAGES.

5. STATUTE: DELAWARE CODE: #3922 & #6104-6105.

6. TYPES OF DAMAGES ALLOWED: DAMAGES TO REAL PROPERTY OF THE VICTIM OR THE VICTIM'S PERSONAL INJURIES.

7. LIMITS ON RECOVERY: $5,000.00 FOR AN ACT OF VANDALISM AND NO LIMIT FOR A VICTIM'S PERSONAL INJURIES.

8. APPLICATION: APPLIES TO ALL JUVENILES UNDER AGE 18.

9. PARTIES RESPONSIBLE: PARENTS OF JUVENILE; LEGAL GUARDIANS APPOINTED BY THE COURT TO OVERSEE THE WELFARE OF THE JUVENILE.

10. ACTION FOR RECOVERY: THE VICTIM FILES A "CIVIL ACTION" IN THE STATE COURT WHERE THE VICTIM LIVES OR WHERE THE PROPERTY IS LOCATED.

FLORIDA

1. ELIGIBILITY: VICTIMS OF JUVENILE CRIMES.

2. CRIME: MUST BE REPORTED TO LOCAL POLICE.

3. CRIMINAL CHARGES: MUST BE FILED WITHIN ONE (1) YEAR.

4. CONVICTION: THE JUVENILE NEED NOT BE CONVICTED OF THE THE CRIME IN ORDER FOR THE VICTIM TO RECOVER DAMAGES.

5. STATUTE: FLORIDA CODE: F.S. #322.09 & F.S. #741.24.

6. TYPES OF DAMAGES ALLOWED: DAMAGES TO REAL PROPERTY OF THE VICTIM OR THE VICTIM'S PERSONAL INJURIES.

7. LIMITS ON RECOVERY: "NO LIMITS" FOR AN ACT OF VANDALISM ON REAL PROPERTY AND "NO LIMITS" FOR PERSONAL INJURIES.

8. APPLICATION: APPLIES TO ALL JUVENILES UNDER AGE 18.

9. PARTIES RESPONSIBLE: PARENTS OF JUVENILE; LEGAL GUARDIANS APPOINTED BY THE COURT TO OVERSEE THE WELFARE OF THE JUVENILE.

10. ACTION FOR RECOVERY: THE VICTIM FILES A "CIVIL ACTION" IN THE STATE COURT WHERE THE VICTIM LIVES OR WHERE THE PROPERTY IS LOCATED.

GEORGIA

1. **ELIGIBILITY: VICTIMS OF JUVENILE CRIMES.**

2. **CRIME: MUST BE REPORTED TO LOCAL POLICE.**

3. **CRIMINAL CHARGES: MUST BE FILED WITHIN ONE (1) YEAR.**

4. **CONVICTION: THE JUVENILE NEED NOT BE CONVICTED OF THE THE CRIME IN ORDER FOR THE VICTIM TO RECOVER DAMAGES.**

5. **STATUTE: GEORGIA CODE: # 51-2-2 & #51-2-3.**

6. **TYPES OF DAMAGES ALLOWED: DAMAGES TO REAL PROPERTY OF THE VICTIM OR THE VICTIM'S PERSONAL INJURIES.**

7. **LIMITS ON RECOVERY: $10,000.00 FOR AN ACT OF VANDALISM AND $10,000.00 FOR A VICTIM'S PERSONAL INJURIES.**

8. **APPLICATION: APPLIES TO ALL JUVENILES UNDER AGE 18.**

9. **PARTIES RESPONSIBLE: PARENTS OF JUVENILE; LEGAL GUARDIANS APPOINTED BY THE COURT TO OVERSEE THE WELFARE OF THE JUVENILE.**

10. **ACTION FOR RECOVERY: THE VICTIM FILES A "CIVIL ACTION" IN THE STATE COURT WHERE THE VICTIM LIVES OR WHERE THE PROPERTY IS LOCATED.**

HAWAII

1. ELIGIBILITY: VICTIMS OF JUVENILE CRIMES.

2. CRIME: MUST BE REPORTED TO LOCAL POLICE.

3. CRIMINAL CHARGES: MUST BE FILED WITHIN ONE (1) YEAR.

4. CONVICTION: THE JUVENILE NEED NOT BE CONVICTED OF THE
THE CRIME IN ORDER FOR THE VICTIM TO RECOVER DAMAGES.

5. STATUTE: HAWAII CODE: #577.3- #577.5 & #286-112.

6. TYPES OF DAMAGES ALLOWED: DAMAGES TO REAL
PROPERTY OF THE VICTIM OR THE VICTIM'S PERSONAL INJURIES.

7. LIMITS ON RECOVERY: "NO LIMITS" FOR AN ACT OF VANDALISM
ON REAL PROPERTY AND "NO LIMITS" FOR PERSONAL INJURIES.

8. APPLICATION: APPLIES TO ALL JUVENILES UNDER AGE 18.

9. PARTIES RESPONSIBLE: PARENTS OF JUVENILE; LEGAL
GUARDIANS APPOINTED BY THE COURT TO OVERSEE THE
WELFARE OF THE JUVENILE.

10. ACTION FOR RECOVERY: THE VICTIM FILES A "CIVIL ACTION"
IN THE STATE COURT WHERE THE VICTIM LIVES OR WHERE
THE PROPERTY IS LOCATED.

IDAHO

1. **ELIGIBILITY: VICTIMS OF JUVENILE CRIMES.**

2. **CRIME: MUST BE REPORTED TO LOCAL POLICE.**

3. **CRIMINAL CHARGES: MUST BE FILED WITHIN ONE (1) YEAR.**

4. **CONVICTION: THE JUVENILE NEED NOT BE CONVICTED OF THE THE CRIME IN ORDER FOR THE VICTIM TO RECOVER DAMAGES.**

5. **STATUTE: IDAHO CODE: #6-210.**

6. **TYPES OF DAMAGES ALLOWED: DAMAGES TO REAL PROPERTY OF THE VICTIM OR THE VICTIM'S PERSONAL INJURIES.**

7. **LIMITS ON RECOVERY: $2,500.00 FOR AN ACT OF VANDALISM AND $2,500.00 FOR A VICTIM'S PERSONAL INJURIES.**

8. **APPLICATION: APPLIES TO ALL JUVENILES UNDER AGE 18.**

9. **PARTIES RESPONSIBLE: PARENTS OF JUVENILE; LEGAL GUARDIANS APPOINTED BY THE COURT TO OVERSEE THE WELFARE OF THE JUVENILE.**

10. **ACTION FOR RECOVERY: THE VICTIM FILES A "CIVIL ACTION" IN THE STATE COURT WHERE THE VICTIM LIVES OR WHERE THE PROPERTY IS LOCATED.**

ILLINOIS

1. ELIGIBILITY: VICTIMS OF JUVENILE CRIMES.

2. CRIME: MUST BE REPORTED TO LOCAL POLICE.

3. CRIMINAL CHARGES: MUST BE FILED WITHIN ONE (1) YEAR.

4. CONVICTION: THE JUVENILE NEED NOT BE CONVICTED OF THE THE CRIME IN ORDER FOR THE VICTIM TO RECOVER DAMAGES.

5. STATUTE: ILLINOIS CODE: #740-115/3 & #5/21-1.2 & #5/16.25.

6. TYPES OF DAMAGES ALLOWED: DAMAGES TO REAL PROPERTY OF THE VICTIM OR THE VICTIM'S PERSONAL INJURIES.

7. LIMITS ON RECOVERY: $20,000.00 FOR AN ACT OF VANDALISM AND $20,000.00 FOR A VICTIM'S PERSONAL INJURIES.

8. APPLICATION: APPLIES TO ALL JUVENILES UNDER AGE 18.

9. PARTIES RESPONSIBLE: PARENTS OF JUVENILE; LEGAL GUARDIANS APPOINTED BY THE COURT TO OVERSEE THE WELFARE OF THE JUVENILE.

10. ACTION FOR RECOVERY: THE VICTIM FILES A "CIVIL ACTION" IN THE STATE COURT WHERE THE VICTIM LIVES OR WHERE THE PROPERTY IS LOCATED.

INDIANA

1. **ELIGIBILITY: VICTIMS OF JUVENILE CRIMES.**

2. **CRIME: MUST BE REPORTED TO LOCAL POLICE.**

3. **CRIMINAL CHARGES: MUST BE FILED WITHIN ONE (1) YEAR.**

4. **CONVICTION: THE JUVENILE NEED NOT BE CONVICTED OF THE THE CRIME IN ORDER FOR THE VICTIM TO RECOVER DAMAGES.**

5. **STATUTE: INDIANA CODE: #34-31-4-1 & #9-24-9-4.**

6. **TYPES OF DAMAGES ALLOWED: DAMAGES TO REAL PROPERTY OF THE VICTIM OR THE VICTIM'S PERSONAL INJURIES.**

7. **LIMITS ON RECOVERY: $5,000.00 FOR AN ACT OF VANDALISM AND NO LIMIT FOR A VICTIM'S PERSONAL INJURIES.**

8. **APPLICATION: APPLIES TO ALL JUVENILES UNDER AGE 18.**

9. **PARTIES RESPONSIBLE: PARENTS OF JUVENILE; LEGAL GUARDIANS APPOINTED BY THE COURT TO OVERSEE THE WELFARE OF THE JUVENILE.**

10. **ACTION FOR RECOVERY: THE VICTIM FILES A "CIVIL ACTION" IN THE STATE COURT WHERE THE VICTIM LIVES OR WHERE THE PROPERTY IS LOCATED.**

IOWA

1. ELIGIBILITY: VICTIMS OF JUVENILE CRIMES.

2. CRIME: MUST BE REPORTED TO LOCAL POLICE.

3. CRIMINAL CHARGES: MUST BE FILED WITHIN ONE (1) YEAR.

4. CONVICTION: THE JUVENILE NEED NOT BE CONVICTED OF THE THE CRIME IN ORDER FOR THE VICTIM TO RECOVER DAMAGES.

5. STATUTE: IOWA CODE: #613.16.

6. TYPES OF DAMAGES ALLOWED: DAMAGES TO REAL PROPERTY OF THE VICTIM OR THE VICTIM'S PERSONAL INJURIES.

7. LIMITS ON RECOVERY: $2,000.00 FOR AN ACT OF VANDALISM AND $5,000.00 FOR A VICTIM'S PERSONAL INJURIES.

8. APPLICATION: APPLIES TO ALL JUVENILES UNDER AGE 18.

9. PARTIES RESPONSIBLE: PARENTS OF JUVENILE; LEGAL GUARDIANS APPOINTED BY THE COURT TO OVERSEE THE WELFARE OF THE JUVENILE.

10. ACTION FOR RECOVERY: THE VICTIM FILES A "CIVIL ACTION" IN THE STATE COURT WHERE THE VICTIM LIVES OR WHERE THE PROPERTY IS LOCATED.

KANSAS

1. ELIGIBILITY: VICTIMS OF JUVENILE CRIMES.

2. CRIME: MUST BE REPORTED TO LOCAL POLICE.

3. CRIMINAL CHARGES: MUST BE FILED WITHIN ONE (1) YEAR.

4. CONVICTION: THE JUVENILE NEED NOT BE CONVICTED OF THE THE CRIME IN ORDER FOR THE VICTIM TO RECOVER DAMAGES.

5. STATUTE: KANSAS CODE: #38-120 & #8-222.

6. TYPES OF DAMAGES ALLOWED: DAMAGES TO REAL PROPERTY OF THE VICTIM OR THE VICTIM'S PERSONAL INJURIES.

7. LIMITS ON RECOVERY: $5,000.00 FOR AN ACT OF VANDALISM AND $5,000.00 FOR A VICTIM'S PERSONAL INJURIES.

8. APPLICATION: APPLIES TO ALL JUVENILES UNDER AGE 18.

9. PARTIES RESPONSIBLE: PARENTS OF JUVENILE; LEGAL GUARDIANS APPOINTED BY THE COURT TO OVERSEE THE WELFARE OF THE JUVENILE.

10. ACTION FOR RECOVERY: THE VICTIM FILES A "CIVIL ACTION" IN THE STATE COURT WHERE THE VICTIM LIVES OR WHERE THE PROPERTY IS LOCATED.

KENTUCKY

1. **ELIGIBILITY: VICTIMS OF JUVENILE CRIMES.**

2. **CRIME: MUST BE REPORTED TO LOCAL POLICE.**

3. **CRIMINAL CHARGES: MUST BE FILED WITHIN ONE (1) YEAR.**

4. **CONVICTION: THE JUVENILE NEED NOT BE CONVICTED OF THE THE CRIME IN ORDER FOR THE VICTIM TO RECOVER DAMAGES.**

5. **STATUTE: KENTUCKY CODE: #305.025 & #186.590(1)-(3).**

6. **TYPES OF DAMAGES ALLOWED: DAMAGES TO REAL PROPERTY OF THE VICTIM OR THE VICTIM'S PERSONAL INJURIES.**

7. **LIMITS ON RECOVERY: $2,500.00 FOR AN ACT OF VANDALISM AND NO LIMIT FOR A VICTIM'S PERSONAL INJURIES.**

8. **APPLICATION: APPLIES TO ALL JUVENILES UNDER AGE 18.**

9. **PARTIES RESPONSIBLE: PARENTS OF JUVENILE; LEGAL GUARDIANS APPOINTED BY THE COURT TO OVERSEE THE WELFARE OF THE JUVENILE.**

10. **ACTION FOR RECOVERY: THE VICTIM FILES A "CIVIL ACTION" IN THE STATE COURT WHERE THE VICTIM LIVES OR WHERE THE PROPERTY IS LOCATED.**

LOUISANA

1. ELIGIBILITY: VICTIMS OF JUVENILE CRIMES.

2. CRIME: MUST BE REPORTED TO LOCAL POLICE.

3. CRIMINAL CHARGES: MUST BE FILED WITHIN ONE (1) YEAR.

4. CONVICTION: THE JUVENILE NEED NOT BE CONVICTED OF THE THE CRIME IN ORDER FOR THE VICTIM TO RECOVER DAMAGES.

5. STATUTE: LOUISANA CODE: ARTICLES: 2318 & 32:417.

6. TYPES OF DAMAGES ALLOWED: DAMAGES TO REAL PROPERTY OF THE VICTIM OR THE VICTIM'S PERSONAL INJURIES.

7. LIMITS ON RECOVERY: NO LIMITS FOR AN ACT OF VANDALISM AND NO LIMITS FOR A VICTIM'S PERSONAL INJURIES.

8. APPLICATION: APPLIES TO ALL JUVENILES UNDER AGE 18.

9. PARTIES RESPONSIBLE: PARENTS OF JUVENILE; LEGAL GUARDIANS APPOINTED BY THE COURT TO OVERSEE THE WELFARE OF THE JUVENILE.

10. ACTION FOR RECOVERY: THE VICTIM FILES A "CIVIL ACTION" IN THE STATE COURT WHERE THE VICTIM LIVES OR WHERE THE PROPERTY IS LOCATED.

MAINE

1. ELIGIBILITY: VICTIMS OF JUVENILE CRIMES.

2. CRIME: MUST BE REPORTED TO LOCAL POLICE.

3. CRIMINAL CHARGES: MUST BE FILED WITHIN ONE (1) YEAR.

4. CONVICTION: THE JUVENILE NEED NOT BE CONVICTED OF THE THE CRIME IN ORDER FOR THE VICTIM TO RECOVER DAMAGES.

5. STATUTE: MAINE CODE: #14-304 & #29A-1651.

6. TYPES OF DAMAGES ALLOWED: DAMAGES TO REAL PROPERTY OF THE VICTIM OR THE VICTIM'S PERSONAL INJURIES.

7. LIMITS ON RECOVERY: $800.00 FOR AN ACT OF VANDALISM AND $800.00 FOR A VICTIM'S PERSONAL INJURIES.

8. APPLICATION: APPLIES TO ALL JUVENILES UNDER AGE 18.

9. PARTIES RESPONSIBLE: PARENTS OF JUVENILE; LEGAL GUARDIANS APPOINTED BY THE COURT TO OVERSEE THE WELFARE OF THE JUVENILE.

10. ACTION FOR RECOVERY: THE VICTIM FILES A "CIVIL ACTION" IN THE STATE COURT WHERE THE VICTIM LIVES OR WHERE THE PROPERTY IS LOCATED.

MARYLAND

1. ELIGIBILITY: VICTIMS OF JUVENILE CRIMES.

2. CRIME: MUST BE REPORTED TO LOCAL POLICE.

3. CRIMINAL CHARGES: MUST BE FILED WITHIN ONE (1) YEAR.

4. CONVICTION: THE JUVENILE NEED NOT BE CONVICTED OF THE THE CRIME IN ORDER FOR THE VICTIM TO RECOVER DAMAGES.

5. STATUTE: MARYLAND CODE: #11-604 & #16-107.

6. TYPES OF DAMAGES ALLOWED: DAMAGES TO REAL PROPERTY OF THE VICTIM OR THE VICTIM'S PERSONAL INJURIES.

7. LIMITS ON RECOVERY: $10,000.00 FOR AN ACT OF VANDALISM AND $10,000.00 FOR A VICTIM'S PERSONAL INJURIES.

8. APPLICATION: APPLIES TO ALL JUVENILES UNDER AGE 18.

9. PARTIES RESPONSIBLE: PARENTS OF JUVENILE; LEGAL GUARDIANS APPOINTED BY THE COURT TO OVERSEE THE WELFARE OF THE JUVENILE.

10. ACTION FOR RECOVERY: THE VICTIM FILES A "CIVIL ACTION" IN THE STATE COURT WHERE THE VICTIM LIVES OR WHERE THE PROPERTY IS LOCATED.

MASSACHUSETTS

1. ELIGIBILITY: VICTIMS OF JUVENILE CRIMES.

2. CRIME: MUST BE REPORTED TO LOCAL POLICE.

3. CRIMINAL CHARGES: MUST BE FILED WITHIN ONE (1) YEAR.

4. CONVICTION: THE JUVENILE NEED NOT BE CONVICTED OF THE

THE CRIME IN ORDER FOR THE VICTIM TO RECOVER DAMAGES.

5. STATUTE: MASSACHUSETTS CODE: #231-85G.

6. TYPES OF DAMAGES ALLOWED: DAMAGES TO REAL

PROPERTY OF THE VICTIM OR THE VICTIM'S PERSONAL INJURIES.

7. LIMITS ON RECOVERY: $5,000.00 FOR AN ACT OF VANDALISM

AND $5,000.00 FOR A VICTIM'S PERSONAL INJURIES.

8. APPLICATION: APPLIES TO ALL JUVENILES UNDER AGE 18.

9. PARTIES RESPONSIBLE: PARENTS OF JUVENILE; LEGAL

GUARDIANS APPOINTED BY THE COURT TO OVERSEE THE

WELFARE OF THE JUVENILE.

10. ACTION FOR RECOVERY: THE VICTIM FILES A "CIVIL ACTION"

IN THE STATE COURT WHERE THE VICTIM LIVES OR WHERE

THE PROPERTY IS LOCATED.

MICHIGAN

1. ELIGIBILITY: VICTIMS OF JUVENILE CRIMES.

2. CRIME: MUST BE REPORTED TO LOCAL POLICE.

3. CRIMINAL CHARGES: MUST BE FILED WITHIN ONE (1) YEAR.

4. CONVICTION: THE JUVENILE NEED NOT BE CONVICTED OF THE THE CRIME IN ORDER FOR THE VICTIM TO RECOVER DAMAGES.

5. STATUTE: MICHIGAN CODE: #231-856.

6. TYPES OF DAMAGES ALLOWED: DAMAGES TO REAL PROPERTY OF THE VICTIM OR THE VICTIM'S PERSONAL INJURIES.

7. LIMITS ON RECOVERY: $2,500.00 FOR AN ACT OF VANDALISM AND $2,500.00 FOR A VICTIM'S PERSONAL INJURIES.

8. APPLICATION: APPLIES TO ALL JUVENILES UNDER AGE 18.

9. PARTIES RESPONSIBLE: PARENTS OF JUVENILE; LEGAL GUARDIANS APPOINTED BY THE COURT TO OVERSEE THE WELFARE OF THE JUVENILE.

10. ACTION FOR RECOVERY: THE VICTIM FILES A "CIVIL ACTION" IN THE STATE COURT WHERE THE VICTIM LIVES OR WHERE THE PROPERTY IS LOCATED.

MINNESOTA

1. ELIGIBILITY: VICTIMS OF JUVENILE CRIMES.

2. CRIME: MUST BE REPORTED TO LOCAL POLICE.

3. CRIMINAL CHARGES: MUST BE FILED WITHIN ONE (1) YEAR.

4. CONVICTION: THE JUVENILE NEED NOT BE CONVICTED OF THE THE CRIME IN ORDER FOR THE VICTIM TO RECOVER DAMAGES.

5. STATUTE: MINNESOTA CODE: #600-2913.

6. TYPES OF DAMAGES ALLOWED: DAMAGES TO REAL PROPERTY OF THE VICTIM OR THE VICTIM'S PERSONAL INJURIES.

7. LIMITS ON RECOVERY: $1,000.00 FOR AN ACT OF VANDALISM AND $5,000.00 FOR A VICTIM'S PERSONAL INJURIES.

8. APPLICATION: APPLIES TO ALL JUVENILES UNDER AGE 18.

9. PARTIES RESPONSIBLE: PARENTS OF JUVENILE; LEGAL GUARDIANS APPOINTED BY THE COURT TO OVERSEE THE WELFARE OF THE JUVENILE.

10. ACTION FOR RECOVERY: THE VICTIM FILES A "CIVIL ACTION" IN THE STATE COURT WHERE THE VICTIM LIVES OR WHERE THE PROPERTY IS LOCATED.

MISSISSIPPI

1. ELIGIBILITY: VICTIMS OF JUVENILE CRIMES.

2. CRIME: MUST BE REPORTED TO LOCAL POLICE.

3. CRIMINAL CHARGES: MUST BE FILED WITHIN ONE (1) YEAR.

4. CONVICTION: THE JUVENILE NEED NOT BE CONVICTED OF THE THE CRIME IN ORDER FOR THE VICTIM TO RECOVER DAMAGES.

5. STATUTE: MISSISSIPPI CODE: #93-13-2, #97-15-1 & #63-1-25.

6. TYPES OF DAMAGES ALLOWED: DAMAGES TO REAL PROPERTY OF THE VICTIM OR THE VICTIM'S PERSONAL INJURIES.

7. LIMITS ON RECOVERY: $5,000.00 FOR AN ACT OF VANDALISM ON REAL PROPERTY AND "NO LIMITS" FOR PERSONAL INJURIES.

8. APPLICATION: APPLIES TO ALL JUVENILES UNDER AGE 18.

9. PARTIES RESPONSIBLE: PARENTS OF JUVENILE; LEGAL GUARDIANS APPOINTED BY THE COURT TO OVERSEE THE WELFARE OF THE JUVENILE.

10. ACTION FOR RECOVERY: THE VICTIM FILES A "CIVIL ACTION" IN THE STATE COURT WHERE THE VICTIM LIVES OR WHERE THE PROPERTY IS LOCATED.

MISSOURI

1. ELIGIBILITY: VICTIMS OF JUVENILE CRIMES.

2. CRIME: MUST BE REPORTED TO LOCAL POLICE.

3. CRIMINAL CHARGES: MUST BE FILED WITHIN ONE (1) YEAR.

4. CONVICTION: THE JUVENILE NEED NOT BE CONVICTED OF THE THE CRIME IN ORDER FOR THE VICTIM TO RECOVER DAMAGES.

5. STATUTE: MISSOURI CODE: #537.045 & #302.250.

6. TYPES OF DAMAGES ALLOWED: DAMAGES TO REAL PROPERTY OF THE VICTIM OR THE VICTIM'S PERSONAL INJURIES.

7. LIMITS ON RECOVERY: $2,000.00 FOR AN ACT OF VANDALISM AND $2,000.00 FOR A VICTIM'S PERSONAL INJURIES.

8. APPLICATION: APPLIES TO ALL JUVENILES UNDER AGE 18.

9. PARTIES RESPONSIBLE: PARENTS OF JUVENILE; LEGAL GUARDIANS APPOINTED BY THE COURT TO OVERSEE THE WELFARE OF THE JUVENILE.

10. ACTION FOR RECOVERY: THE VICTIM FILES A "CIVIL ACTION" IN THE STATE COURT WHERE THE VICTIM LIVES OR WHERE THE PROPERTY IS LOCATED.

MONTANA

1. ELIGIBILITY: VICTIMS OF JUVENILE CRIMES.

2. CRIME: MUST BE REPORTED TO LOCAL POLICE.

3. CRIMINAL CHARGES: MUST BE FILED WITHIN ONE (1) YEAR.

4. CONVICTION: THE JUVENILE NEED NOT BE CONVICTED OF THE THE CRIME IN ORDER FOR THE VICTIM TO RECOVER DAMAGES.

5. STATUTE: MONTANA CODE: #40-6-237 & #61-5-108

6. TYPES OF DAMAGES ALLOWED: DAMAGES TO REAL PROPERTY OF THE VICTIM OR THE VICTIM'S PERSONAL INJURIES.

7. LIMITS ON RECOVERY: $2,500.00 FOR AN ACT OF VANDALISM AND $2,500.00 FOR A VICTIM'S PERSONAL INJURIES.

8. APPLICATION: APPLIES TO ALL JUVENILES UNDER AGE 18.

9. PARTIES RESPONSIBLE: PARENTS OF JUVENILE; LEGAL GUARDIANS APPOINTED BY THE COURT TO OVERSEE THE WELFARE OF THE JUVENILE.

10. ACTION FOR RECOVERY: THE VICTIM FILES A "CIVIL ACTION" IN THE STATE COURT WHERE THE VICTIM LIVES OR WHERE THE PROPERTY IS LOCATED.

NEBRASKA

1. **ELIGIBILITY: VICTIMS OF JUVENILE CRIMES.**

2. **CRIME: MUST BE REPORTED TO LOCAL POLICE.**

3. **CRIMINAL CHARGES: MUST BE FILED WITHIN ONE (1) YEAR.**

4. **CONVICTION: THE JUVENILE NEED NOT BE CONVICTED OF THE THE CRIME IN ORDER FOR THE VICTIM TO RECOVER DAMAGES.**

5. **STATUTE: NEBRASKA CODE: #43-801.**

6. **TYPES OF DAMAGES ALLOWED: DAMAGES TO REAL PROPERTY OF THE VICTIM OR THE VICTIM'S PERSONAL INJURIES.**

7. **LIMITS ON RECOVERY: $1,000.00 FOR AN ACT OF VANDALISM AND $1,000.00 FOR A VICTIM'S PERSONAL INJURIES.**

8. **APPLICATION: APPLIES TO ALL JUVENILES UNDER AGE 18.**

9. **PARTIES RESPONSIBLE: PARENTS OF JUVENILE; LEGAL GUARDIANS APPOINTED BY THE COURT TO OVERSEE THE WELFARE OF THE JUVENILE.**

10. **ACTION FOR RECOVERY: THE VICTIM FILES A "CIVIL ACTION" IN THE STATE COURT WHERE THE VICTIM LIVES OR WHERE THE PROPERTY IS LOCATED.**

NEVADA

1. **ELIGIBILITY: VICTIMS OF JUVENILE CRIMES.**

2. **CRIME: MUST BE REPORTED TO LOCAL POLICE.**

3. **CRIMINAL CHARGES: MUST BE FILED WITHIN ONE (1) YEAR.**

4. **CONVICTION: THE JUVENILE NEED NOT BE CONVICTED OF THE THE CRIME IN ORDER FOR THE VICTIM TO RECOVER DAMAGES.**

5. **STATUTE: NEVADA CODE: #41-470-472 & #483.300.**

6. **TYPES OF DAMAGES ALLOWED: DAMAGES TO REAL PROPERTY OF THE VICTIM OR THE VICTIM'S PERSONAL INJURIES.**

7. **LIMITS ON RECOVERY: $10,000.00 FOR AN ACT OF VANDALISM ON REAL PROPERTY AND "NO LIMITS" FOR PERSONAL INJURIES.**

8. **APPLICATION: APPLIES TO ALL JUVENILES UNDER AGE 18.**

9. **PARTIES RESPONSIBLE: PARENTS OF JUVENILE; LEGAL GUARDIANS APPOINTED BY THE COURT TO OVERSEE THE WELFARE OF THE JUVENILE.**

10. **ACTION FOR RECOVERY: THE VICTIM FILES A "CIVIL ACTION" IN THE STATE COURT WHERE THE VICTIM LIVES OR WHERE THE PROPERTY IS LOCATED.**

NEW HAMPSHIRE

1. ELIGIBILITY: VICTIMS OF JUVENILE CRIMES.

2. CRIME: MUST BE REPORTED TO LOCAL POLICE.

3. CRIMINAL CHARGES: MUST BE FILED WITHIN ONE (1) YEAR.

4. CONVICTION: THE JUVENILE NEED NOT BE CONVICTED OF THE THE CRIME IN ORDER FOR THE VICTIM TO RECOVER DAMAGES.

5. STATUTE: NEW HAMPSHIRE CODE: #507-8-E

6. TYPES OF DAMAGES ALLOWED: DAMAGES TO REAL OR PROPERTY OWNED BY THE VICTIM.

7. LIMITS ON RECOVERY: NO LIMITS FOR AN ACT OF VANDALISM AND NO LIMITS FOR AN AUTO ACCIDENT INVOLVING THE JUVENILE.

8. APPLICATION: APPLIES TO ALL JUVENILES UNDER AGE 18.

9. PARTIES RESPONSIBLE: PARENTS OF JUVENILE; LEGAL GUARDIANS APPOINTED BY THE COURT TO OVERSEE THE WELFARE OF THE JUVENILE.

10. ACTION FOR RECOVERY: THE VICTIM FILES A "CIVIL ACTION" IN THE STATE COURT WHERE THE VICTIM LIVES OR WHERE THE PROPERTY IS LOCATED.

NEW YORK

1. ELIGIBILITY: VICTIMS OF JUVENILE CRIMES.

2. CRIME: MUST BE REPORTED TO LOCAL POLICE.

3. CRIMINAL CHARGES: MUST BE FILED WITHIN ONE (1) YEAR.

4. CONVICTION: THE JUVENILE NEED NOT BE CONVICTED OF THE THE CRIME IN ORDER FOR THE VICTIM TO RECOVER DAMAGES.

5. STATUTE: NEW YORK CODE: #3-112(1)

6. TYPES OF DAMAGES ALLOWED: DAMAGES TO REAL PROPERTY OF THE VICTIM OR THE VICTIM'S PERSONAL INJURIES.

7. LIMITS ON RECOVERY: $5,000.00 FOR AN ACT OF VANDALISM ON REAL PROPERTY AND $5,000.00 FOR THEFT OF PROPERTY.

8. APPLICATION: APPLIES TO ALL JUVENILES UNDER AGE 18.

9. PARTIES RESPONSIBLE: PARENTS OF JUVENILE; LEGAL GUARDIANS APPOINTED BY THE COURT TO OVERSEE THE WELFARE OF THE JUVENILE.

10. ACTION FOR RECOVERY: THE VICTIM FILES A "CIVIL ACTION" IN THE STATE COURT WHERE THE VICTIM LIVES OR WHERE THE PROPERTY IS LOCATED.

OHIO

1. ELIGIBILITY: VICTIMS OF JUVENILE CRIMES.

2. CRIME: MUST BE REPORTED TO LOCAL POLICE.

3. CRIMINAL CHARGES: MUST BE FILED WITHIN ONE (1) YEAR.

4. CONVICTION: THE JUVENILE NEED NOT BE CONVICTED OF THE THE CRIME IN ORDER FOR THE VICTIM TO RECOVER DAMAGES.

5. STATUTE: OHIO CODE: #2307.07, #3109.09-10 & #4507.07.

6. TYPES OF DAMAGES ALLOWED: DAMAGES TO REAL PROPERTY OF THE VICTIM OR THE VICTIM'S PERSONAL INJURIES.

7. LIMITS ON RECOVERY: $15,000.00 FOR AN ACT OF VANDALISM ON REAL PROPERTY AND "NO LIMITS" FOR PERSONAL INJURIES.

8. APPLICATION: APPLIES TO ALL JUVENILES UNDER AGE 18.

9. PARTIES RESPONSIBLE: PARENTS OF JUVENILE; LEGAL GUARDIANS APPOINTED BY THE COURT TO OVERSEE THE WELFARE OF THE JUVENILE.

10. ACTION FOR RECOVERY: THE VICTIM FILES A "CIVIL ACTION" IN THE STATE COURT WHERE THE VICTIM LIVES OR WHERE THE PROPERTY IS LOCATED.

NEW JERSEY

1. ELIGIBILITY: VICTIMS OF JUVENILE CRIMES.

2. CRIME: MUST BE REPORTED TO LOCAL POLICE.

3. CRIMINAL CHARGES: MUST BE FILED WITHIN ONE (1) YEAR.

4. CONVICTION: THE JUVENILE NEED NOT BE CONVICTED OF THE THE CRIME IN ORDER FOR THE VICTIM TO RECOVER DAMAGES.

5. STATUTE: NEW JERSEY CODE: #2A.53A-16 & 18A-37-3.

6. TYPES OF DAMAGES ALLOWED: DAMAGES TO REAL PROPERTY OF THE VICTIM OR THE VICTIM'S PERSONAL INJURIES.

7. LIMITS ON RECOVERY: $5,000.00 FOR AN ACT OF VANDALISM FOR PRIVATE PROPERTY & NO LIMITS--PUBLIC PROPERTY DAMAGE.

8. APPLICATION: APPLIES TO ALL JUVENILES UNDER AGE 18.

9. PARTIES RESPONSIBLE: PARENTS OF JUVENILE; LEGAL GUARDIANS APPOINTED BY THE COURT TO OVERSEE THE WELFARE OF THE JUVENILE.

10. ACTION FOR RECOVERY: THE VICTIM FILES A "CIVIL ACTION" IN THE STATE COURT WHERE THE VICTIM LIVES OR WHERE THE PROPERTY IS LOCATED.

NEW MEXICO

1. ELIGIBILITY: VICTIMS OF JUVENILE CRIMES.

2. CRIME: MUST BE REPORTED TO LOCAL POLICE.

3. CRIMINAL CHARGES: MUST BE FILED WITHIN ONE (1) YEAR.

4. CONVICTION: THE JUVENILE NEED NOT BE CONVICTED OF THE THE CRIME IN ORDER FOR THE VICTIM TO RECOVER DAMAGES.

5. STATUTE: NEW MEXICO CODE: #32A-2-27 & #66-5-11.

6. TYPES OF DAMAGES ALLOWED: DAMAGES TO REAL PROPERTY OF THE VICTIM OR THE VICTIM'S PERSONAL INJURIES.

7. LIMITS ON RECOVERY: $4,000.00 FOR AN ACT OF VANDALISM AND NO LIMIT FOR A VICTIM'S PERSONAL INJURIES.

8. APPLICATION: APPLIES TO ALL JUVENILES UNDER AGE 18.

9. PARTIES RESPONSIBLE: PARENTS OF JUVENILE; LEGAL GUARDIANS APPOINTED BY THE COURT TO OVERSEE THE WELFARE OF THE JUVENILE.

10. ACTION FOR RECOVERY: THE VICTIM FILES A "CIVIL ACTION" IN THE STATE COURT WHERE THE VICTIM LIVES OR WHERE THE PROPERTY IS LOCATED.

NORTH CAROLINA

1. **ELIGIBILITY: VICTIMS OF JUVENILE CRIMES.**

2. **CRIME: MUST BE REPORTED TO LOCAL POLICE.**

3. **CRIMINAL CHARGES: MUST BE FILED WITHIN ONE (1) YEAR.**

4. **CONVICTION: THE JUVENILE NEED NOT BE CONVICTED OF THE THE CRIME IN ORDER FOR THE VICTIM TO RECOVER DAMAGES.**

5. **STATUTE: NORTH CAROLINA CODE: #1-538-1.**

6. **TYPES OF DAMAGES ALLOWED: DAMAGES TO REAL PROPERTY OF THE VICTIM OR THE VICTIM'S PERSONAL INJURIES.**

7. **LIMITS ON RECOVERY: $2,000.00 FOR AN ACT OF VANDALISM AND $2,000.00 FOR A VICTIM'S PERSONAL INJURIES.**

8. **APPLICATION: APPLIES TO ALL JUVENILES UNDER AGE 18.**

9. **PARTIES RESPONSIBLE: PARENTS OF JUVENILE; LEGAL GUARDIANS APPOINTED BY THE COURT TO OVERSEE THE WELFARE OF THE JUVENILE.**

10. **ACTION FOR RECOVERY: THE VICTIM FILES A "CIVIL ACTION" IN THE STATE COURT WHERE THE VICTIM LIVES OR WHERE THE PROPERTY IS LOCATED.**

NORTH DAKOTA

1. ELIGIBILITY: VICTIMS OF JUVENILE CRIMES.

2. CRIME: MUST BE REPORTED TO LOCAL POLICE.

3. CRIMINAL CHARGES: MUST BE FILED WITHIN ONE (1) YEAR.

4. CONVICTION: THE JUVENILE NEED NOT BE CONVICTED OF THE THE CRIME IN ORDER FOR THE VICTIM TO RECOVER DAMAGES.

5. STATUTE: NORTH DAKOTA CODE: #32-03-39 & 39-06-09.

6. TYPES OF DAMAGES ALLOWED: DAMAGES TO REAL PROPERTY OF THE VICTIM OR THE VICTIM'S PERSONAL INJURIES.

7. LIMITS ON RECOVERY: $1,000.00 FOR AN ACT OF VANDALISM AND NO LIMIT FOR A VICTIM'S PERSONAL INJURIES.

8. APPLICATION: APPLIES TO ALL JUVENILES UNDER AGE 18.

9. PARTIES RESPONSIBLE: PARENTS OF JUVENILE; LEGAL GUARDIANS APPOINTED BY THE COURT TO OVERSEE THE WELFARE OF THE JUVENILE.

10. ACTION FOR RECOVERY: THE VICTIM FILES A "CIVIL ACTION" IN THE STATE COURT WHERE THE VICTIM LIVES OR WHERE THE PROPERTY IS LOCATED.

OKLAHOMA

1. ELIGIBILITY: VICTIMS OF JUVENILE CRIMES.

2. CRIME: MUST BE REPORTED TO LOCAL POLICE.

3. CRIMINAL CHARGES: MUST BE FILED WITHIN ONE (1) YEAR.

4. CONVICTION: THE JUVENILE NEED NOT BE CONVICTED OF THE THE CRIME IN ORDER FOR THE VICTIM TO RECOVER DAMAGES.

5. STATUTE: OKLAHOMA CODE: 23 O.S. # 10 & 47 O.S. # 607.

6. TYPES OF DAMAGES ALLOWED: DAMAGES TO REAL PROPERTY OF THE VICTIM OR THE VICTIM'S PERSONAL INJURIES.

7. LIMITS ON RECOVERY: $2,500.00 FOR AN ACT OF VANDALISM AND $2,500.00 FOR A VICTIM'S PERSONAL INJURIES.

8. APPLICATION: APPLIES TO ALL JUVENILES UNDER AGE 18.

9. PARTIES RESPONSIBLE: PARENTS OF JUVENILE; LEGAL GUARDIANS APPOINTED BY THE COURT TO OVERSEE THE WELFARE OF THE JUVENILE.

10. ACTION FOR RECOVERY: THE VICTIM FILES A "CIVIL ACTION" IN THE STATE COURT WHERE THE VICTIM LIVES OR WHERE THE PROPERTY IS LOCATED.

OREGON

1. **ELIGIBILITY: VICTIMS OF JUVENILE CRIMES.**

2. **CRIME: MUST BE REPORTED TO LOCAL POLICE.**

3. **CRIMINAL CHARGES: MUST BE FILED WITHIN ONE (1) YEAR.**

4. **CONVICTION: THE JUVENILE NEED NOT BE CONVICTED OF THE THE CRIME IN ORDER FOR THE VICTIM TO RECOVER DAMAGES.**

5. **STATUTE: OREGON CODE: #30.765.**

6. **TYPES OF DAMAGES ALLOWED: DAMAGES TO REAL PROPERTY OF THE VICTIM OR THE VICTIM'S PERSONAL INJURIES.**

7. **LIMITS ON RECOVERY: $7,500.00 FOR AN ACT OF VANDALISM AND $7,500.00 FOR A VICTIM'S PERSONAL INJURIES.**

8. **APPLICATION: APPLIES TO ALL JUVENILES UNDER AGE 18.**

9. **PARTIES RESPONSIBLE: PARENTS OF JUVENILE; LEGAL GUARDIANS APPOINTED BY THE COURT TO OVERSEE THE WELFARE OF THE JUVENILE.**

10. **ACTION FOR RECOVERY: THE VICTIM FILES A "CIVIL ACTION" IN THE STATE COURT WHERE THE VICTIM LIVES OR WHERE THE PROPERTY IS LOCATED.**

PENNSYLVANIA

1. ELIGIBILITY: VICTIMS OF JUVENILE CRIMES.

2. CRIME: MUST BE REPORTED TO LOCAL POLICE.

3. CRIMINAL CHARGES: MUST BE FILED WITHIN ONE (1) YEAR.

4. CONVICTION: THE JUVENILE NEED NOT BE CONVICTED OF THE
THE CRIME IN ORDER FOR THE VICTIM TO RECOVER DAMAGES.

5. STATUTE: PENNSYLVANIA CODE: 23 P.C. #5502-5505.

6. TYPES OF DAMAGES ALLOWED: DAMAGES TO REAL
PROPERTY OF THE VICTIM OR THE VICTIM'S PERSONAL INJURIES.

7. LIMITS ON RECOVERY: $1,000.00 FOR AN ACT OF VANDALISM
ON REAL PROPERTY AND $2,500.00 FOR PERSONAL INJURIES.

8. APPLICATION: APPLIES TO ALL JUVENILES UNDER AGE 18.

9. PARTIES RESPONSIBLE: PARENTS OF JUVENILE; LEGAL
GUARDIANS APPOINTED BY THE COURT TO OVERSEE THE
WELFARE OF THE JUVENILE.

10. ACTION FOR RECOVERY: THE VICTIM FILES A "CIVIL ACTION"
IN THE STATE COURT WHERE THE VICTIM LIVES OR WHERE
THE PROPERTY IS LOCATED.

RHODE ISLAND

1. ELIGIBILITY: VICTIMS OF JUVENILE CRIMES.

2. CRIME: MUST BE REPORTED TO LOCAL POLICE.

3. CRIMINAL CHARGES: MUST BE FILED WITHIN ONE (1) YEAR.

4. CONVICTION: THE JUVENILE NEED NOT BE CONVICTED OF THE THE CRIME IN ORDER FOR THE VICTIM TO RECOVER DAMAGES.

5. STATUTE: RHODE ISLAND CODE: 1956-#9-1-3.

6. TYPES OF DAMAGES ALLOWED: DAMAGES TO REAL OR PROPERTY OWNED BY THE VICTIM OR PERSONAL INJURIES.

7. LIMITS ON RECOVERY: $1,500.00 FOR AN ACT OF VANDALISM AND $1,500.00 FOR AN MULTIPLE ACTS INVOLVING THE JUVENILE.

8. APPLICATION: APPLIES TO ALL JUVENILES UNDER AGE 18.

9. PARTIES RESPONSIBLE: PARENTS OF JUVENILE; LEGAL GUARDIANS APPOINTED BY THE COURT TO OVERSEE THE WELFARE OF THE JUVENILE.

10. ACTION FOR RECOVERY: THE VICTIM FILES A "CIVIL ACTION" IN THE STATE COURT WHERE THE VICTIM LIVES OR WHERE THE PROPERTY IS LOCATED.

SOUTH CAROLINA

1. **ELIGIBILITY: VICTIMS OF JUVENILE CRIMES.**

2. **CRIME: MUST BE REPORTED TO LOCAL POLICE.**

3. **CRIMINAL CHARGES: MUST BE FILED WITHIN ONE (1) YEAR.**

4. **CONVICTION: THE JUVENILE NEED NOT BE CONVICTED OF THE THE CRIME IN ORDER FOR THE VICTIM TO RECOVER DAMAGES.**

5. **STATUTE: SOUTH CAROLINA CODE: #63-5-60 & #31-10-15.**

6. **TYPES OF DAMAGES ALLOWED: DAMAGES TO REAL PROPERTY OF THE VICTIM OR THE VICTIM'S PERSONAL INJURIES.**

7. **LIMITS ON RECOVERY: $5,000.00 FOR AN ACT OF VANDALISM AND $5,000.00 FOR A VICTIM'S PERSONAL INJURIES.**

8. **APPLICATION: APPLIES TO ALL JUVENILES UNDER AGE 18.**

9. **PARTIES RESPONSIBLE: PARENTS OF JUVENILE; LEGAL GUARDIANS APPOINTED BY THE COURT TO OVERSEE THE WELFARE OF THE JUVENILE.**

10. **ACTION FOR RECOVERY: THE VICTIM FILES A "CIVIL ACTION" IN THE STATE COURT WHERE THE VICTIM LIVES OR WHERE THE PROPERTY IS LOCATED.**

SOUTH DAKOTA

1. ELIGIBILITY: VICTIMS OF JUVENILE CRIMES.

2. CRIME: MUST BE REPORTED TO LOCAL POLICE.

3. CRIMINAL CHARGES: MUST BE FILED WITHIN ONE (1) YEAR.

4. CONVICTION: THE JUVENILE NEED NOT BE CONVICTED OF THE THE CRIME IN ORDER FOR THE VICTIM TO RECOVER DAMAGES.

5. STATUTE: SOUTH DAKOTA CODE: # 25-5-15.

6. TYPES OF DAMAGES ALLOWED: DAMAGES TO REAL PROPERTY OF THE VICTIM OR THE VICTIM'S PERSONAL INJURIES.

7. LIMITS ON RECOVERY: $2,500.00 FOR AN ACT OF VANDALISM AND $2,500.00 FOR A VICTIM'S PERSONAL INJURIES.

8. APPLICATION: APPLIES TO ALL JUVENILES UNDER AGE 18.

9. PARTIES RESPONSIBLE: PARENTS OF JUVENILE; LEGAL GUARDIANS APPOINTED BY THE COURT TO OVERSEE THE WELFARE OF THE JUVENILE.

10. ACTION FOR RECOVERY: THE VICTIM FILES A "CIVIL ACTION" IN THE STATE COURT WHERE THE VICTIM LIVES OR WHERE THE PROPERTY IS LOCATED.

TENNESSEE

1. ELIGIBILITY: VICTIMS OF JUVENILE CRIMES.

2. CRIME: MUST BE REPORTED TO LOCAL POLICE.

3. CRIMINAL CHARGES: MUST BE FILED WITHIN ONE (1) YEAR.

4. CONVICTION: THE JUVENILE NEED NOT BE CONVICTED OF THE THE CRIME IN ORDER FOR THE VICTIM TO RECOVER DAMAGES.

5. STATUTE: TENNESSEE CODE: #37-10-101 & 55-50-312.

6. TYPES OF DAMAGES ALLOWED: DAMAGES TO REAL PROPERTY OF THE VICTIM OR THE VICTIM'S PERSONAL INJURIES.

7. LIMITS ON RECOVERY: $10,000.00 FOR AN ACT OF VANDALISM AND NO LIMIT FOR A VICTIM'S PERSONAL INJURIES.

8. APPLICATION: APPLIES TO ALL JUVENILES UNDER AGE 18.

9. PARTIES RESPONSIBLE: PARENTS OF JUVENILE; LEGAL GUARDIANS APPOINTED BY THE COURT TO OVERSEE THE WELFARE OF THE JUVENILE.

10. ACTION FOR RECOVERY: THE VICTIM FILES A "CIVIL ACTION" IN THE STATE COURT WHERE THE VICTIM LIVES OR WHERE THE PROPERTY IS LOCATED.

TEXAS

1. ELIGIBILITY: VICTIMS OF JUVENILE CRIMES.

2. CRIME: MUST BE REPORTED TO LOCAL POLICE.

3. CRIMINAL CHARGES: MUST BE FILED WITHIN ONE (1) YEAR.

4. CONVICTION: THE JUVENILE NEED NOT BE CONVICTED OF THE THE CRIME IN ORDER FOR THE VICTIM TO RECOVER DAMAGES.

5. STATUTE: TEXAS CODE: #41-001 AND #41-002

6. TYPES OF DAMAGES ALLOWED: DAMAGES TO REAL PROPERTY OF THE VICTIM OR THE VICTIM'S PERSONAL INJURIES.

7. LIMITS ON RECOVERY: $25,000.00 FOR AN ACT OF VANDALISM ON REAL PROPERTY AND $25,000.00 FOR PERSONAL INJURIES.

8. APPLICATION: APPLIES TO ALL JUVENILES UNDER AGE 18.

9. PARTIES RESPONSIBLE: PARENTS OF JUVENILE; LEGAL GUARDIANS APPOINTED BY THE COURT TO OVERSEE THE WELFARE OF THE JUVENILE.

10. ACTION FOR RECOVERY: THE VICTIM FILES A "CIVIL ACTION" IN THE STATE COURT WHERE THE VICTIM LIVES OR WHERE THE PROPERTY IS LOCATED.

UTAH

1. **ELIGIBILITY: VICTIMS OF JUVENILE CRIMES.**

2. **CRIME: MUST BE REPORTED TO LOCAL POLICE.**

3. **CRIMINAL CHARGES: MUST BE FILED WITHIN ONE (1) YEAR.**

4. **CONVICTION: THE JUVENILE NEED NOT BE CONVICTED OF THE THE CRIME IN ORDER FOR THE VICTIM TO RECOVER DAMAGES.**

5. **STATUTE: UTAH CODE: #1953-78 & #1953-3-211-212.**

6. **TYPES OF DAMAGES ALLOWED: DAMAGES TO REAL PROPERTY OF THE VICTIM OR THE VICTIM'S PERSONAL INJURIES.**

7. **LIMITS ON RECOVERY: $2,000.00 FOR AN ACT OF VANDALISM AND NO LIMIT FOR A VICTIM'S PERSONAL INJURIES.**

8. **APPLICATION: APPLIES TO ALL JUVENILES UNDER AGE 18.**

9. **PARTIES RESPONSIBLE: PARENTS OF JUVENILE; LEGAL GUARDIANS APPOINTED BY THE COURT TO OVERSEE THE WELFARE OF THE JUVENILE.**

10. **ACTION FOR RECOVERY: THE VICTIM FILES A "CIVIL ACTION" IN THE STATE COURT WHERE THE VICTIM LIVES OR WHERE THE PROPERTY IS LOCATED.**

VERMONT

1. **ELIGIBILITY: VICTIMS OF JUVENILE CRIMES.**

2. **CRIME: MUST BE REPORTED TO LOCAL POLICE.**

3. **CRIMINAL CHARGES: MUST BE FILED WITHIN ONE (1) YEAR.**

4. **CONVICTION: THE JUVENILE NEED NOT BE CONVICTED OF THE THE CRIME IN ORDER FOR THE VICTIM TO RECOVER DAMAGES.**

5. **STATUTE: VERMONT CODE: 15 # 901**

6. **TYPES OF DAMAGES ALLOWED: DAMAGES TO REAL OR PROPERTY OWNED BY THE VICTIM OR PERSONAL INJURIES.**

7. **LIMITS ON RECOVERY: $5,000.00 FOR AN ACT OF VANDALISM AND $5,000.00 FOR AN MULTIPLE ACTS INVOLVING THE JUVENILE.**

8. **APPLICATION: APPLIES TO ALL JUVENILES UNDER AGE 18.**

9. **PARTIES RESPONSIBLE: PARENTS OF JUVENILE; LEGAL GUARDIANS APPOINTED BY THE COURT TO OVERSEE THE WELFARE OF THE JUVENILE.**

10. **ACTION FOR RECOVERY: THE VICTIM FILES A "CIVIL ACTION" IN THE STATE COURT WHERE THE VICTIM LIVES OR WHERE THE PROPERTY IS LOCATED.**

VIRGINIA

1. **ELIGIBILITY: VICTIMS OF JUVENILE CRIMES.**

2. **CRIME: MUST BE REPORTED TO LOCAL POLICE.**

3. **CRIMINAL CHARGES: MUST BE FILED WITHIN ONE (1) YEAR.**

4. **CONVICTION: THE JUVENILE NEED NOT BE CONVICTED OF THE THE CRIME IN ORDER FOR THE VICTIM TO RECOVER DAMAGES.**

5. **STATUTE: VIRGINIA CODE: #8.01-43, #8.01-44 & #8.01.64.**

6. **TYPES OF DAMAGES ALLOWED: DAMAGES TO REAL PROPERTY OF THE VICTIM OR THE VICTIM'S PERSONAL INJURIES.**

7. **LIMITS ON RECOVERY: $2,500.00 FOR AN ACT OF VANDALISM AND $2,500.00 FOR A VICTIM'S PERSONAL INJURIES.**

8. **APPLICATION: APPLIES TO ALL JUVENILES UNDER AGE 18.**

9. **PARTIES RESPONSIBLE: PARENTS OF JUVENILE; LEGAL GUARDIANS APPOINTED BY THE COURT TO OVERSEE THE WELFARE OF THE JUVENILE.**

10. **ACTION FOR RECOVERY: THE VICTIM FILES A "CIVIL ACTION" IN THE STATE COURT WHERE THE VICTIM LIVES OR WHERE THE PROPERTY IS LOCATED.**

WASHINGTON

1. **ELIGIBILITY: VICTIMS OF JUVENILE CRIMES.**

2. **CRIME: MUST BE REPORTED TO LOCAL POLICE.**

3. **CRIMINAL CHARGES: MUST BE FILED WITHIN ONE (1) YEAR.**

4. **CONVICTION: THE JUVENILE NEED NOT BE CONVICTED OF THE THE CRIME IN ORDER FOR THE VICTIM TO RECOVER DAMAGES.**

5. **STATUTE: WASHINGTON CODE: #4.24.190**

6. **TYPES OF DAMAGES ALLOWED: DAMAGES TO REAL OR PROPERTY OWNED BY THE VICTIM OR PERSONAL INJURIES.**

7. **LIMITS ON RECOVERY: $5,000.00 FOR AN ACT OF VANDALISM AND $5,000.00 FOR AN MULTIPLE ACTS INVOLVING THE JUVENILE.**

8. **APPLICATION: APPLIES TO ALL JUVENILES UNDER AGE 18.**

9. **PARTIES RESPONSIBLE: PARENTS OF JUVENILE; LEGAL GUARDIANS APPOINTED BY THE COURT TO OVERSEE THE WELFARE OF THE JUVENILE.**

10. **ACTION FOR RECOVERY: THE VICTIM FILES A "CIVIL ACTION" IN THE STATE COURT WHERE THE VICTIM LIVES OR WHERE THE PROPERTY IS LOCATED.**

WEST VIRGINIA

1. ELIGIBILITY: VICTIMS OF JUVENILE CRIMES.

2. CRIME: MUST BE REPORTED TO LOCAL POLICE.

3. CRIMINAL CHARGES: MUST BE FILED WITHIN ONE (1) YEAR.

4. CONVICTION: THE JUVENILE NEED NOT BE CONVICTED OF THE THE CRIME IN ORDER FOR THE VICTIM TO RECOVER DAMAGES.

5. STATUTE: WEST VIRGINIA CODE: #55-7A.2

6. TYPES OF DAMAGES ALLOWED: DAMAGES TO REAL OR PROPERTY OWNED BY THE VICTIM OR PERSONAL INJURIES.

7. LIMITS ON RECOVERY: $5,000.00 FOR AN ACT OF VANDALISM AND $5,000.00 FOR AN AUTO ACCIDENT INVOLVING THE JUVENILE.

8. APPLICATION: APPLIES TO ALL JUVENILES UNDER AGE 18.

9. PARTIES RESPONSIBLE: PARENTS OF JUVENILE; LEGAL GUARDIANS APPOINTED BY THE COURT TO OVERSEE THE WELFARE OF THE JUVENILE.

10. ACTION FOR RECOVERY: THE VICTIM FILES A "CIVIL ACTION" IN THE STATE COURT WHERE THE VICTIM LIVES OR WHERE THE PROPERTY IS LOCATED.

WISCONSIN

1. ELIGIBILITY: VICTIMS OF JUVENILE CRIMES.

2. CRIME: MUST BE REPORTED TO LOCAL POLICE.

3. CRIMINAL CHARGES: MUST BE FILED WITHIN ONE (1) YEAR.

4. CONVICTION: THE JUVENILE NEED NOT BE CONVICTED OF THE THE CRIME IN ORDER FOR THE VICTIM TO RECOVER DAMAGES.

5. STATUTE: WISCONSIN CODE: #895-035 & #343.15

6. TYPES OF DAMAGES ALLOWED: DAMAGES TO REAL PROPERTY OF THE VICTIM OR THE VICTIM'S PERSONAL INJURIES.

7. LIMITS ON RECOVERY: $5,000.00 FOR AN ACT OF VANDALISM AND NO LIMIT FOR A VICTIM'S PERSONAL INJURIES.

8. APPLICATION: APPLIES TO ALL JUVENILES UNDER AGE 18.

9. PARTIES RESPONSIBLE: PARENTS OF JUVENILE; LEGAL GUARDIANS APPOINTED BY THE COURT TO OVERSEE THE WELFARE OF THE JUVENILE.

10. ACTION FOR RECOVERY: THE VICTIM FILES A "CIVIL ACTION" IN THE STATE COURT WHERE THE VICTIM LIVES OR WHERE THE PROPERTY IS LOCATED.

WYOMING

1. ELIGIBILITY: VICTIMS OF JUVENILE CRIMES.

2. CRIME: MUST BE REPORTED TO LOCAL POLICE.

3. CRIMINAL CHARGES: MUST BE FILED WITHIN ONE (1) YEAR.

4. CONVICTION: THE JUVENILE NEED NOT BE CONVICTED OF THE THE CRIME IN ORDER FOR THE VICTIM TO RECOVER DAMAGES.

5. STATUTE: WYOMING CODE: #14-2-203

6. TYPES OF DAMAGES ALLOWED: DAMAGES TO REAL OR PROPERTY OWNED BY THE VICTIM.

7. LIMITS ON RECOVERY: $2,000.00 FOR AN ACT OF VANDALISM ON PROPERTY OWNED BY THE VICTIM.

8. APPLICATION: APPLIES TO ALL JUVENILES UNDER AGE 18.

9. PARTIES RESPONSIBLE: PARENTS OF JUVENILE; LEGAL GUARDIANS APPOINTED BY THE COURT TO OVERSEE THE WELFARE OF THE JUVENILE.

10. ACTION FOR RECOVERY: THE VICTIM FILES A "CIVIL ACTION" IN THE STATE COURT WHERE THE VICTIM LIVES OR WHERE THE PROPERTY IS LOCATED.

STATE LAWS ON THE PARENTAL LIABILITY

FOR ACTIONS OF JUVENILE CHILDREN

ALABAMA: ALABAMA CODE, #6—5—380(1975).

ALASKA: ALASKA CODE, #09.65.255 & 28.15.071.

ARIZONA: ARIZONIA CODE, # 12.661.

ARKANSAS: ARKANSAS CODE, #09—25—102.

CALIFORNIA: CALIFORNIA CODE, #1714. 1-3 & #17707-17708.

COLORADO: COLORADO CODE: #13-21-107-107.5 & #42-2-108/

CONECTICUT: CONNECTICUT CODE: #52-572.

DELAWARE: DELAWARE CODE: # 3922 #6104-6105.

FLORIDA: FLORIDA CODE: F.S. #322.09 & F.S. #741.24.

GEROGIA: GEORGIA CODE: #51-2-2 & #51-2-3.

HAWAII: HAWAII CODE: #577.3-& #577.5 & #286-112.

IDAHO: IDAHO CODE: #6-210.

ILLINOIS: ILLINOIS CODE: #740-115.3 & #5/21, & #5/16.25.

INDIANA: INDIANA CODE: #34-31-4-1 & #9-24-9-4.

IOWA: IOWA CODE: #613.16.

KANSAS: KANSAS CODE: #38-120 & #8-222.

KENTUCKY: KENTUCKY CODE: #305.025 & 186.590.1-186.590.3.

LOUISANA: LOUISANA CODE: ARTICLES: 2318 & 32-417.

MAINE: MAINE CODE: #13-304 & 29A-1651.

PARENTAL LIABILITY LAWS (CONTINUED):

MARYLAND: MARYLAND CODE: #11-604 & #16-107.

MASSACHUSETTS, MASSACHUSETTS CODE: #231-85G.

MICHIGAN, MICHIGAN CODE: #231-856.

MINNESOTA, MINNESOTA CODE: #600-2913.

MISSISSIPPI, MISSISSIPPI CODE: #93-13.2 #97-15-1 & #63.1-25.

MISSOURI, MISSOURI CODE: #537.045 & #302.250.

MONTANA, MONTANA CODE: #40-6-237 & #61-5-108.

NEBRASKA, NEBRASKA CODE: #43-801.

NEVADA, NEVADA CODE: #41-470-472 & #483.300.

NEW HAMPSHIRE, NEW HAMPSHIRE CODE: #507-8-E.

NEW YORK, NEW YORK CODE: #3-112(1).

OHIO, OHIO CODE: #2307.07. #3109.09-10 & #4507.07.

NEW JERSEY, NEW JERSEY CODE: #2A.53A-16 & 18A.-37.3.

NEW MEXICO, NEW MEXICO CODE: 32A-2.27 & #66-5-11.

NORTH CAROLINA, NORTH CAROLINA CODE: #1-538-1.

NORTH DAKOTA, NORTH DAKOTA CODE: #32-03-39 & 39-06-09.

OKLAHOMA, OKLAHOMA CODE: 23 O.S. #10 & 47 O.S. #607.

OREGON, OREGON CODE: #30.765.

PENNSYLVANIA, PENNSYLVANIA CODE: 23 P.C. #5502-5505.

RHODE IDLAND, RHODE ISLAND CODE: 1956-#9-1-3.

PARENTAL LIABILITY LAWS (CONTINUED):

SOUTH CAROLINA, SOUTH CAROLINA CODE: #63-5-60 & #31-10-15.

SOUTH DAKOTA, SOUTH DAKOTA CODE: # 25-5-15.

TENNESSEE, TENNESSEE CODE: #37-10-101 & #55-5—312.

TEXAS, TEXAS CODE: #41-001 & #41-002.

UTAH, UTAH CODE: #1953-78 & 1953-3-211-212.

VERMONT, VERMONT CODE: #15 & #901.

VIRGINIA, VIRGINIA CODE: #8.01-43, #8.01-44 & #8.01.64.

WASHINGTON, WASHINGTON CODE: #4.24.190.

WEST VIRGINIA, WEST VIRGINIA CODE: #55-7A.2.

WISCONSIN, WISCONSIN CODE: #895-035 % #343.15.

WYOMING, WYOMING CODE: #14.2.203.

BIBLIOGRAPHY

A. PAYNE V. TENNESSEE, 501 U.S. 808 (1991).

B. MAPP V. OHIO, 367 U.S. 644 (1961).

C. GIDEON V. WAINWRIGHT, 372 U.S. 335 (1963).

D. MIRANDA V. ARIZONA, 384 U.S. 436 (1966).

E. IN RE GAULT, 387 U.S. 1 (1967).

F. IN RE WINSHIP, 397 U.S. 358 (1970).

G. THOMPSON V. OKLAHOMA, 487 U.S. 815 (1988).

H. SELLERS V. WARD, 135 F.3D 1333, (1998).

I. SIMMONS V. ROPER, 543 U.S. 551 (2005).

J. MCKEIVER V. PENNSYLVANIA, 403 U.S. 528 (1971).

K. A.B.A. INSTITUTE ON JUVENILE JUSTICE, (2000).

L. KENT V. U.S. GOV'T, 383 U.S. 86, (1966).

M. BREED V. JONES, 421 U.S. 519, (1975).

N. DAILY OKLAHOMAN V. OKLAHOMA, 480 U.S. 308 (1977)

O. SMITH V. THE DAILY MAIL, 443 U.S. 97 (1979).

P. SCHALL V. MARTIN, 467 U.S. 253 (1984).

Q. GRAHAM V. FLORIDA, 130 U.S.S.CT. 2011 (2010).

R. MILLER V. ALABAMA, 567 U.S. 460, (2012).

S. J.D.B. V. NORTH CAROLINA, 131 U.S.S.CT. 2394 (2011).

CPSIA information can be obtained
at www.ICGtesting.com
Printed in the USA
LVHW100113191218
601011LV00014B/834/P